Keeping my

MANDARIN
Alive

Keeping my MANDARIN Alive

LEE KUAN YEW'S

Language
Learning
Experience

edited by **CHUA Chee Lay**

National Institute of Education
Nanyang Technological University

World Scientific

八方文化
Global Publishing Co. Pte. Ltd
创 作 室

Published by

World Scientific Publishing Co. Pte. Ltd.
and
Global Publishing Co. Pte. Ltd.
5 Toh Tuck Link, Singapore 596224
USA office: 27 Warren Street, Suite 401-402, Hackensack, NJ 07601
UK office: 57 Shelton Street, Covent Garden, London WC2H 9HE

Advisers: Seng Han Thong, Chew Cheng Hai
Editor: Chua Chee Lay
Acquisition & Desk Editor: Ho Sheo Be
Editor of eBook: Lee Choin Lan
Designer: Ho Bee Keow
Typesetter: Amy Lee
DVD Production: Bider Singapore Pte Ltd
Photography: Lance Lee/Acht! Studios (unless otherwise stated)
Video-recording: RayCine Productions

Front Cover:
Minister Mentor Lee Kuan Yew against a language exercise designed by his tutor of 30 years, Professor Chew Cheng Hai.

KEEPING MY MANDARIN ALIVE: Lee Kuan Yew's Language Learning Experience

© 2005 Lee Kuan Yew

ISBN   981-256-402-0
ISBN   981-256-382-2 (pbk)

Printed in Singapore by KHL Printing Co. Pte. Ltd.

Contents ●v

vi Preface

1 Quotable Quotes

13 Interview with Minister Mentor
Lee Kuan Yew

120 Quotable Quotes

142 Teaching Chinese to Adults
An Interview with MM Lee's Chinese Language Tutor,
Professor Chew Cheng Hai

160 Learn as We Teach
An Interview with MM Lee's Chinese Language Tutor,
Dr Chua Chee Lay

172 Relating Chinese to English
An Interview with MM Lee's Chinese Language Tutor,
Dr Goh Yeng Seng

184 Learning Materials

224 Some Useful Resources for
Chinese Language Learning

234 Epilogue

Preface

Chua Chee Lay

National Institute of Education,
Nanyang Technological University, Singapore
1 May 2005

"Everything would be worthwhile if I can set a good example for others to follow and encourage them to learn Chinese."

These words from Minister Mentor (MM) Lee Kuan Yew underscore the objective of this publication — to provide an insight into his journey of acquiring the Chinese language so that others may draw lessons from his experience and strategies.

Many of us are familiar with the political ideology and economic policy of MM Lee. However, few of us know his language learning tactics, including using the latest digital technologies. Many of us know that he has been taking Mandarin lessons for many years,

but only a few know how committed and diligent he is in his Mandarin lessons.

For the first time, MM Lee shares the difficulties he faces as an adult student of the Chinese language and how he overcame the difficulties (he started learning Mandarin only at the age of 32 and Hokkien at age 38). In this book, he candidly recounts how he learnt Mandarin during the last 50 years and how he keeps up with it. He also tells when and why he decided to learn the language, where he got his learning materials, from whom he learnt his Mandarin and what spurred him on this learning journey for more than half a century.

This is not a book of MM Lee's language theory or his language policy. Instead, it is a detailed description of his Chinese language learning journey, one that is fraught with difficulties and obstacles. During this 50-year journey, he has held steadfast to his belief that as a Chinese he must be able to speak and understand the Chinese language. To him, keeping his Chinese language alive is not solely for economic reasons but also to give him a sense of identity and pride in the culture and civilisation of our Chinese ancestors. His advice to both the younger generation and their parents is loud and clear: learn the language when you are young. Keep it alive for the rest of your life.

MM Lee advises that to be an effective and efficient language student, we must set a realistic learning goal and understand our own learning style. It is also important for us to understand the usage of the target language, analyse and be conscious of the strengths and weaknesses of our language learning ability.

In this book, MM Lee illustrates how he sets his language goal after analysing his language ability and how he monitors the progress of his learning systematically. His main aim now is to be able to convert his large repertoire of passive Mandarin vocabulary into active and ready-to-use words.

MM Lee pays special attention to the standard pronunciation of Mandarin. He feels that if we have to learn Mandarin, we should learn to speak **standard** Mandarin. This is his own language expectation and requirement. Hence, he has always insisted that those who speak good Mandarin be his Mandarin teachers so that they can serve as his language model. To him, a good language teacher who is able to answer queries and clear doubts is essential.

MM Lee also noticed that Chinese computing has flourished after decades of research and development. As end-users, it is timely for us to grab this golden opportunity and take full advantage of these powerful digital language tools to maximise our learning and mastering of the Chinese language. We must also not forget that a conducive environment is essential for the language to grow. In addition, we need to remember that it is only with frequent usage that the language can be kept alive.

Acknowledgements

I am privileged to be invited as the editor of this publication. Its completion, however, would not be possible without the assistance and advice of my mentors, friends and colleagues.

I am greatly indebted to Minister Mentor Lee Kuan Yew for his kindness and support throughout this project. His candid sharing and insightful comments have made this project a very special and meaningful one.

The two advisers for this project, Member of Parliament Mr Seng Han Thong who has always been concerned about the development of the Chinese language, and Professor Chew Cheng Hai, the main Chinese language tutor of Minister Mentor Lee for the past 30 years, have also provided me with invaluable advice.

This project would not have been possible without the support and assistance of Professor Phua Kok Khoo (Executive Chairman and CEO, World Scientific Publishing Company), Ms Yeong Yoon Ying (Press Secretary to Minister Mentor) and Mr Chen Jian Min (CEO, Bider Technology Pte Ltd, Singapore), the sponsor of the eBook of this project.

Staff from World Scientific Publishing Company, desk editors Miss Ho Sheo Be and Miss Chung Poh Leng, and graphic designer Ms Ho Bee Keow have helped make my editorial task a breeze with their tenacity and professionalism. My grateful thanks also to my research partner, Mr Lee Choin Lan (Lecturer, National Institute of Education), whom I have roped in to be the editor of the eBook, for his innovative ideas and achieving a technological breakthrough by complementing this publication with an eBook.

Above all, I wish to thank my wife Huey Pyng, who has always supported me in all aspects of life, including this project, and to my three-year-old daughter, Annabelle, whose bedtime story sessions had to be shortened so that I could complete this project.

About the Editor

Dr Chua is a third generation Singaporean born and bred in Singapore. He is a Chinese linguist, educational technology researcher, award-wining poet and a dedicated teacher who has been commended Excellence in Teaching. He received an overseas scholarship from Nanyang Technological University (NTU) to pursue his MA and PhD in Chinese Linguistics at the University of Wisconsin-Madison in the US. He is the Chinese language tutor for Minister Mentor Lee Kuan Yew, as well as the President of the Republic of Singapore, His Excellency S R Nathan, and the Minister for Defence, Rear Admiral Teo Chee Hean. Dr Chua is now the Head of Chinese Language Learning Technologies Research Lab based in National Institute of Education, NTU, Singapore.

Keeping my

Mandarin

Alive

Quotable Quotes

Values [

It is not just learning the language. With the language goes the fables and proverbs. It is learning a whole value system, a whole philosophy of life, that can maintain the fabric of our society, in spite of exposure to all the current madness around the world.

5 Nov 1972

Discomfiture

Only a Chinese Singaporean who cannot speak or read it, and who has been exposed to discomfiture or ridicule when abroad, will know how inadequate and how deprived he can feel. By then, they would not be young enough to learn the language easily. I have personally experienced this.

21 Sep 1984

Quebec/Belgium

Were it possible for people to use two languages with equal facility, then the language problem of Quebec (French and English) or of Belgium (French and Flemish) would not exist. If the Canadians and Belgians have difficulties reconciling two working languages, both European languages and both using the Roman alphabet, **we must be realistic when setting the standards of English and Chinese**, two totally unrelated languages, that we teach in schools.

26 Dec 1989

A Living Language

At the working level, in daily life, I do not see Mandarin becoming obsolete because nobody is using it. It's not possible. The habits will remain. The markets, hawker centres, supermarkets, they will use Mandarin. But you don't have to have high-level Mandarin. You can get by with about 2000 words. That keeps it a living language.

Mandarin: The Chinese Connection, 2000

9

Widespread Usage

Given that we wanted the bulk of our Chinese Singaporeans to achieve reasonable proficiency in Chinese language, we had to create a widespread need to use Chinese language. For our students, Chinese language has to be a "live" language, as opposed to a classroom subject.

17 Jul 2004

11

Interview

with Minister Mentor

Lee Kuan Yew

by *Ho Sheo Be*

19, 26 Mar 2005

Istana

? Minister Mentor, we noticed that you have collected a lot of notes on your Chinese lessons over the years, is this a special effort and why?

They were left in case at some time or other I wanted to look up something which I had learnt; they are there but not easily retrievable. They became too voluminous and there was no computer to hold them as digital files which were easily retrievable. But they should be useful because they show in writing the amount of materials that I had gone through.

?

What you have laid out on the table today is certainly just a small part of the materials you have gone through. I believe you started to learn Chinese as early as during the Japanese occupation, perhaps you would like to share with us the experience?

The Early Years

I started to learn Chinese in 1942, probably in March or April. The Japanese captured Singapore in February and suddenly the notices were in Japanese, in *kanji*. I didn't want to learn Japanese because I disliked them; they were very brutal. So I decided to learn Chinese to understand what they were writing. I bought several "Chinese taught through English" books from bookshops in Bras Basah Road. I found two sets. One was *Mandarin Made Easy* by Chiang Ker Chiu, then intermediate Mandarin and advanced Mandarin — teaching Mandarin through English. Next, there was a set

> I was very particular that if I had to learn, I wanted to learn the correct pronunciation and not a dialect pronunciation...

of four books from the Prinsep Street Chinese School, teaching Chinese using English. After each lesson, there was a glossary explaining the Chinese characters in English. I spent about six to eight months going through them all. Nothing else to do, just sat down at home to self study. I mastered about 2000 characters, but in a superficial way. I only knew the meaning of the characters and that a combination of the characters meant something else. I didn't learn to pronounce the words, because I had no teacher.

Looking back now, I think I made a mistake. If I had looked for a teacher, I would have found one. I had a neighbour living opposite me who was the nephew of a civil servant called Lee Siow Mong. He came over to teach me. He was a *Chaozhou ren* [潮州人, Teochew] (chuckles). His Mandarin had *Chaozhou de qiang diao* [潮州的腔调, a Teochew accent]. I was very particular that if I had to learn, I

wanted to learn the correct pronunciation and not a dialect pronunciation, so I erased this teaching. Then I became a clerk at a Japanese textile firm. I had to copy Japanese words — *katakana, hiragana* and *kanji*. So my writing in kanji was consolidated. I also learnt touch typing with a Pitman's book. But I did not keep up my Chinese; I just read *kanji* which was necessary to understand Japanese.

I came back (from England) to Singapore in 1950. By 1951/52, I started to learn Mandarin. I learnt it with my friend Hon Sui Sen.[1] We got a man who was supposed to have a Beijing accent. We made some progress but it was not a serious effort, because the lessons were conducted in the evenings — two or three times a week. We tape-recorded him on a very small Grundig tape recorder with a spool tape. It was a dictaphone. The reproduction was very poor. The teacher got suspicious because once (the lessons were) recorded, he thought we would not need him (chuckles). He wasn't keen on re-cording. He wasn't very successful, so we dropped him.

That lasted for probably about eight or nine months. That gave me a slight basis and revived my memory of the *kanji*. Then in 1955, I contested elections in Tanjong Pagar. There were two opponents, one was a Raffles College boy whom I know,[2] the other was Lam

---

[1] Hon Sui Sen (1916–1983) was Singapore's Finance Minister and one of the architects of the country's economic miracle.

[2] Established in 1928, Raffles College provided tertiary level education in the liberal arts and sciences until 1949 when it merged with the King Edward VII Medical College to form the University of Malaya.

Lee Kuan Yew studying by the fireplace at Cambridge *(archived photograph from MM Lee)*.

Tian. He was from Chinese High School, a Hakka like me. He challenged me to a debate in Mandarin in Tanjong Pagar which included at that time Niu Che Shui [牛车水, Chinatown]. Of course it could have been a calamity for me and so I evaded him. It was my first shock and I had to make a speech at a rally in Banda Street. About 30,000 to 40,000 people crammed into the square where today the Kreta Ayer Theatre is. I got hold of a journalist called Jek Yuen Thong to assist me.[3] He was a *Sin Pao* journalist.[4] I said, "Jek, write me a short speech in Mandarin." And he did one page. I practised very hard for a few days (laughs). He used one phrase: that we were honest people, that we were an honest party, and the others were not trustworthy — that they were *gua yang tou mai gou rou* [挂羊头卖狗肉, to palm off something inferior to what it purported to be] — so I practised that speech.

---

[3] Jek Yuen Thong later became Lee Kuan Yew's political secretary and a minister in his government.
[4] *Sin Pao* was a left-wing broadsheet.

You knew what that meant?

Yes, of course. I knew what I was saying, I was worried I could not pronounce it properly. The crowd knew that I was learning, so they cheered me — it went well. Then I picked up Mandarin. The (party) branches grew very rapidly. As the secretary-general of the party, I had to meet many Chinese-educated, young workers. Many of them were left-wingers who spoke either dialect or Mandarin. So I decided to concentrate on Mandarin because there are so many dialects. Every day at lunchtime in my office at Malacca Street, my branch activist, who I think was a pro-communist left-winger, would come to teach me for about one hour. As I progressed, he brought me a little

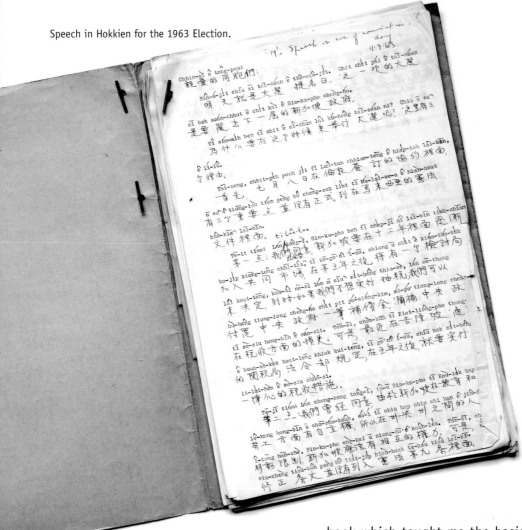

book which taught me the basic words and phrases that the communists used, Marxist philosophy. It was called *Ren Sheng Guan* [《人生观》, *Outlook on Life*]. I don't know whether it is still available, it was my first primer on communist politics.

By 1955/59, I could make speeches in Mandarin without difficulty, but of course I was always looking for new words and phrases, because my English vocabulary was much bigger than my Chinese.

"Gin Nah Mai Chio, Wah Bei Oh"

Then came another shock. In 1961, we had to fight the by-election in Hong Lim and that was a Hokkien-speaking area, China Street. Ong Eng Guan, Singapore's first and last mayor, was our party's treasurer and a Minister for National Development. He clashed with us, he wanted to be the boss, so he started denouncing us. He then resigned (his seat in Hong Lim) and fought the by-election. We knew that we needed a Hokkien speaker. The other Hokkien speaker we had was Lim Chin Siong,[5] but Lim Chin Siong was not with us anymore. We did not trust him. My colleagues,

[5] A leader among the Chinese-educated activists who belonged to the working class, Lim Chin Siong formed the *Barisan Sosialis* or "Socialist Front", a breakaway faction of the People's Action Party (PAP), in Malaya in 1961.

That was life and death.

especially Dr Goh (Keng Swee),[6] said, "You learn Hokkien." (laughs) I just said, "Okay, I'll learn Hokkien." I had Mandarin, it was a great help. I learnt to change the pronunciation into Hokkien, except that many (Hokkien) words have no characters. It was a tremendous effort. At the first meeting, the children laughed at me. I said, *"Gin nah mai chio, wah bei oh,"* [in Hokkien, it means "kids don't laugh, I want to learn"] and that I am learning and I have something serious to tell you.

The election went on for about three months, we dragged it out because I needed time to learn my Hokkien and to get my ideas across. By the end of the three months, I could make a simple speech in Hokkien because every day when I spoke, this Radio Singapore reporter — I think he was a reporter but later he became an editor — Sia Cheng Tit who was a great

---

[6] Another of Lee Kuan Yew's "Old Guard" whose portfolio included Minister of Defence, Minister of Finance, and Deputy Prime Minister, among others.

enthusiast, would listen to me while I spoke in English. He knew that I had wanted to say in Hokkien and was looking for the Mandarin and Hokkien words. He noted them down and would turn up the next day at lunch with the words and phrases all with the romanised pronunciation and with the tones (Hokkien has seven tones). He was educated in *wen yan* [文言, classical Chinese], so he is very fond of beautiful, eight-character apho-

rism. I learnt them by heart (laughs).

That was life and death. If I did not master that, I could not have won the referendum in 1962[7]; I could not have gone throughout Singapore in 1963 to *fang wen* [访问, visit the people]; I could not have won the elections. So, every National Day rally I would speak in Hokkien because that was the language that got the biggest audience. To do a National Day Rally

---

[7] Referendum on whether to merge with Malaysia.

You cannot learn English and Mandarin and speak dialects at home at the same time — it's not possible.

speech in Hokkien without a script, to express my political ideas for about 40 minutes, I had to master several new words and phrases. To make sure that I mastered them, I would make similar speeches at several community centres before that. Mr Sia would listen to me, correct me and get it exactly right, so that by the time I got on television, I would be almost word perfect. Because I switched to Hokkien, Mandarin became secondary. But we were teaching students in schools Mandarin, so

they saw the Prime Minister speaking Hokkien and said, "Nothing wrong, we carry on in Hokkien." So, they were not mastering Mandarin. The Education Ministry brought this problem up to me. I decided to stop (using) Hokkien.

My last speech in Hokkien was made in 1979 and from then on, I spoke Mandarin. (I was telling the people) not to speak dialects at all but learn Mandarin. You cannot learn English and Mandarin and speak

dialects at home at the same time — it's not possible. I know it's not possible because it takes up more brain space, more "megabytes" in the brain. Every word in Hokkien is pronounced differently from Mandarin, the sound is different. "*Hai zi*" [孩子, children] becomes "*gin nah*"; "*nü zi*" [女子, woman] becomes "*cha bo*" — it's complicated. I switched back to Mandarin.

Specialised Mandarin

The Mandarin that I learnt was special for what I had to say. The words that I know best are the ideas that I wanted to put across either on politics, the economy, society or whatever. For what you'd call *ying chou hua* [应酬话 or social conversation], supposing someone spoke about issues on "*bao jian*" [保健, healthcare], I had to find the answer to that. *Han xuan* [寒暄, exchange of greetings] cannot be done. There's a big lapse even today.

Have you succeeded in picking up words in areas other than politics and economics over the years?

(Laughs) I am trying, but it is not easy because it does not come naturally. I used to meet Taiwanese ministers. They had old-school education, so to speak, and used very flowery phrases, I felt very embarrassed that I could not reply in the same way.

Then I found this man, Yu Hou [尉厚], a Mainlander Taiwanese who came here in the 1960s to teach our announcers and teachers the correct pronunciation. If we had to learn Mandarin, let's not speak Nanyang *pu tong hua* [普通话, literally common speech of the Chinese language] but *biao*

Let's not speak Nanyang *pu tong hua* but *biao zhun hua yu*.

zhun hua yu [标准华语, standard Mandarin]. So we got the Chinese teachers from Taiwan, to polish the Mandarin of our teachers and announcers. Because we did that, today the standard of Mandarin in Singapore is more *biao zhun* [standard]. For my own teachers, I always chose people who spoke *biao zhun* (Mandarin). I cannot speak *biao zhun* (Mandarin) but know when it is *biao zhun*. I get introductions to people who are good.

Were you worried about the political cost of giving up Hokkien as many people were then still speaking dialects?

I had a responsibility not to mislead the young. As long as I was still speaking Hokkien at the National Day Rally, I was in fact saying it's okay to do so. If so, they [the people] would never give up Hokkien; they would never move to Mandarin. So the Speak Mandarin Campaign would fail and the learning of Mandarin in schools would never be successful.[8] So, never mind the price, *yi shen zuo ze* [以身作则, setting a good example], it had to be done. Everyone has a limit; you have to decide what do you want to do within your limited capacity and how do you maximise it for your life?

---

[8] The Speak Mandarin Campaign was launched by the then Prime Minister Lee Kuan Yew in 1979 to transform a deeply entrenched social-linguistic habit of Chinese Singaporeans who were long used to the speaking of dialects.

You have not seen any example of people who speak good dialects, English and Mandarin?

Very few, Seng Han Thong is one but he is an interpreter.[9] He has a specially trained capability and an in-born skill. For the average person, to master two languages is already a problem. Let me put it simply this way and I am speaking from my own experience, watching my children, my friends and generally testing people who are bilingual and trilingual. If I only learn English and, say, I reach 100%, when I learn Malay, Mandarin and Hokkien, I cannot score 100% in each. The more I learn for the next language, the lower my score in my first language. I say to Singaporeans:

---

[9] Seng Han Thong is a Member of Parliament and an Assistant Secretary-General of the National Trade Union Congress of Singapore.

Your hard disk is only one gigabyte, what you put in pushes out something else.

You decide, if you want good Chinese, you must be prepared to let your English go down to 90, 80 odd percent. Then, you can reach 50, 60 or 70% in Chinese. Or, you can go to Chinese schools and do English as a second language, then your Chinese can go up to 80%, and your English will go down to 50 or 60%. Very few can do both at the same level; 100% for each, I'd say that's possible only for a few who are specially gifted. I have spoken to many interpreters on what they do to keep their two languages up, particularly those who interpret for me in China.

(Once), after a trip in Beijing, we went on a plane to different provinces. I asked them [the interpreters] how had they kept up with their English. They said they read, listened to tapes, and if they didn't interpret and didn't read, then they were unable to keep it up. So, to do that, you have to push many things out of your mind. I have learnt six languages: English, Malay, Latin (to pass my examinations in school so that I could study law), then I learnt Chinese, Japanese and Hokkien. If you can take the example of a computer: your hard disk is only one gigabyte, what you put in pushes out something else. As you grow older, your gigabyte reduces, because every year, after the age of 20, you lose 1 million neurons. So you've got to delete.

After I retired from Prime Minister-ship, I went to Japan. Whilst talking to the Japanese through an interpreter, I could understand snatches of what they said because at the end of the Japanese occu-pation in September 1945, I was able to be an interpreter for business purposes. During a trip to Japan, I decided to re-learn Japanese. The Ambassador bought me some books, I brought them home and started reading. After a while, I said, "No, I am a stupid man, I meet a Japanese once in a month or once in two months and he brings an interpreter, when I bring it [Japanese] back into my hard disk, I am pushing out something else." So I stopped.

We have to make our minds up, parents must understand this: we must make a living in Singapore, we have decided and, I think rightly, that English is our working language. Otherwise, Singapore would divide, clash, collide, collapse. Non-Chinese would not be able to survive. So, how do we keep Chinese alive? And it is very important that we keep Chinese, not just for economic reasons, but for reasons of identity, sense of self, and pride in our own culture and civilisation.

The motivation behind your effort in learning Mandarin appears to have been primarily political. With a changing environment, particularly as more of the voters are now conversant in English, why have you persevered in the effort to learn Mandarin? What moves you on?

Because I have not forgotten my sense of loss.

Whilst I was in England (after Liberation), I felt a

deep sense of loss that I did not know Chinese.

There was a club called the China Institute in

Gordon Square financed by the Boxer Indemnity

Fund which the British had extracted from the

Chinese government. That club was open to all

Chinese from anywhere in the world. As students,

we were very poor. They gave me what they'd call

high tea, meaning a semi-dinner — sandwiches,

tea, and a few cakes. So, I could skip dinner and

save money. I used to meet Chinese from all over

the world. After a while, I could tell the difference

All of Lee Kuan Yew's three children, including his eldest son Lee Hsien Loong (centre), were educated in Nanyang Primary School, a traditional Chinese school *(archived photograph from MM Lee)*.

between a Singapore or Malayan Chinese, Hong Kong Chinese, China Chinese, Carribean Chinese, Mauritian Chinese — most were from the British empire. Those who were most de-culturalised were from the West Indies, because they

Whilst I was in England, I felt a deep sense of loss that I did not know Chinese.

were farthest away from China. They couldn't speak dialect, their connection with China had been lost.

When I used to go to hotels to register, they would say, "Oh, Chinese," so I thought it was a deep loss that I could not speak or understand Chinese.

That's why I sent my children to Chinese schools. I think from the age of three, my wife had a Chinese teacher to teach them at home. Then at the age of five, they were sent to Nanyang You Zhi Yuan [南

洋幼稚园] (now it's called You Er Yuan [幼儿园]) [Nanyang Kindergarten], and then Nanyang Xiao Xue [南洋小学, Nanyang Primary School]. For the eldest, he had Chinese education right up to *gao zhong er* [高中二, second year of pre-university], for a total of 12 years. The other two had 10 years of Chinese education. At home I used to speak to them in Mandarin to practise my Mandarin and they learnt English from their mother and from books. But in the end, English became their master

Having spent all this effort, I am determined not to lose it.

language, because they went on to English language universities and they use English every day (instead of) Mandarin. But they already have it [Chinese] deeply implanted in their brains so that it can be easily revived. In their case, it was like a sapling, with deep roots, but in my case, it was like an instant tree chopped off from the ground; not so stable, the roots not so deep.

If today I am unable to read the Chinese characters on the wall or the newspapers, I'd feel I am inadequate. I read three times faster in English than I read in Chinese. Sometimes the (Chinese) word is so small, I am not sure what the word is. In English, I can scan the whole sentence; in Chinese, if I miss one or two characters, I cannot be sure of the meaning. I will feel a sense of loss and having spent all this effort, I am determined not to lose it. It is as simple as that.

?

What do you now do to keep up your Mandarin?

Every day I'll read the newspapers for 10 to 15 minutes, no time. I am not reading the news because all the news which is important, I'd have already read them in the English newspapers. I want to see how they [the Chinese press] present the news, the captions, and what they consider important, then I read specific portions like the editorial comments, letters, commentaries, local commentaries, and news on China, Taiwan or Hong Kong which is not in the English press. But that's passive; just looking at the characters and not speaking. My problem now is that once I stopped being the Prime Minister, I am not making as many

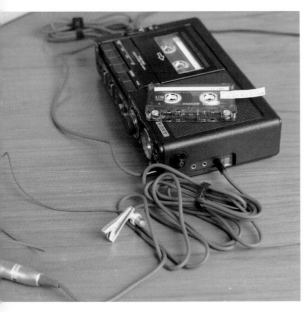

The recorder that MM Lee uses to record his Chinese lessons.

speeches. The quickest way I learnt was when I had to make a speech. I have to translate the words, the phrases I need, then I have to memorise them and use them. Because I use them, they get deeper in. Now I am just reading the newspapers, it's passive learning, not active. But it keeps it [Chinese] up.

I have lessons once a week — not really lessons, just sessions to keep the conversation up, widen my knowledge of contemporary words and phrases. When I am shaving and I am brushing my teeth, I have the tape on to listen to what I've been discussing with my teachers. Again it is passive, *xiao ji de* [消极的]. Finally when you stand up (to make a speech), you have to speak out the words. That means it must be in the active part of your vocabulary — on immediate recall,

Learn young ... capture the fluency, capture the way you speak it, capture the grammar ...

on the hard disk. That's the difference being on the hard disk and on the CD-ROM. I know the word but to speak it out when I have to, if somebody gives me a cue, yes, it will come back but not instantaneously.

So, these are limitations which we must accept. I am convinced that, if I had to re-educate myself from primary school again, knowing that I come from an English-speaking background, I'd go straight into a Chinese school, do six years of

Chinese to get it deep into me, then switch to English with Chinese as a second language, but I would keep it up and never lose touch with it.

When my son went to Cambridge, England, at the age of 20, I knew he would no longer speak Mandarin, so I told him to take along with him some Chinese novels to read and keep his familiarity with the words. After he came back here, he worked in English. When he entered politics in 1984, he had to warm up his Mandarin again, but it came back easily because it was embedded deep in his hard disk. Even so, after taking a budget through Parliament, when he meets the press, or people at a *dui hua hui* [对话会, dialogue], he has to learn the financial words and phrases because he has been using English phrases. It's just not possible to be 100% in one language and 100% in the other, even 90 in one and 90 in the other is difficult, unless you are doing nothing else but interpreting. The average person has got a job, he's concentrating on either law, medicine, politics, economics or business.

Learn young, never mind the standard, capture the fluency, capture the way you speak it, capture the grammar, never mind if your vocabulary is limited, you can expand it later on.

Lee Kuan Yew has been seizing every opportunity to learn Mandarin, and no exception was made even when he was having his vacation in the Cameron Highlands *(archived photograph from MM Lee)*.

For those passive words and phrases, how do you revise them or find ways to use them?

I've got so much, it's just not possible to revise. There are always new words, new phrases. You see, SARS [severe acute respiratory syndrome] took place, you had (earlier) learnt haze, *yin mai* [阴霾] and you started reading about it every day in the newspapers. You have to move on, your needs move on.

When I first went to China, I had to learn a whole series of Chinese names and acronyms, phrases like *wen hua da ge ming* [文化大革命, Cultural Revolution] is *wen ge* [文革]. I don't use them now, they can be revived but what for? Your needs move with the change in the subject that you are talking about and you have to prepare for it.

After I left Malaysia, I concentrated on English and Mandarin. Now very seldom do I make speeches in Malay. When I had to meet Suharto,[10] I would listen to his tapes, his speeches, to refresh my memory of his accent, the way he pronounced words and the words he used. So, when I met him, I had no difficulty understanding him, although I had difficulty finding words to express myself because I had not been using them. There is a difference between passive and active vocabulary. Passive you'd just register, you understand; active, you've to get it in your active vocabulary. You must be able to express yourself, find the right words, put them in the right order and then your meaning comes through.

[10] Former President of Indonesia who ruled the country from 1967 to 1998.

First visit to China in 1976 *(archived photograph from MM Lee)*.

What about seizing opportunities to practise speaking Mandarin, how do you do that now?

That is my problem, as I get older, I am not socialising so much. In the old days, I used to meet the Chinese-speaking MPs [Members of Parliament], Chinese reporters or grassroots leaders and I would automatically speak Mandarin to them. Now, when I go to the community centres, more than 50% of the people speak English because the language environment has changed. People who speak Mandarin to me are the older people; the younger people speak English, they learnt CL2 [Chinese as a Second

Language]. Furthermore, we've got Indians, Eurasians and others, they will feel excluded. When they are around, we have to speak in English. The language environment, inevitably, makes us use English more than any other language. I think we must make an effort to create language situations where Chinese meet and speak Mandarin.

We must make an effort to create language situations where Chinese meet and speak Mandarin.

?

In learning Mandarin, what were some difficulties that you encountered and how did you overcome them?

Pronunciation was (learnt) very early on, once I captured the pronunciation and I knew the *zhu yin fu hao* [注音符号],[11] I didn't worry about the pronunciation any more. I knew how not to follow my earlier teachers' or tutors' pronunciation because I knew their Mandarin was with dialect accents. I'll tell you one strange situation. When I was in China for the first time in 1976, they had a very good interpreter, she was very competent. Then we went to Guangzhou, (where) the Vice

---

[11] *Zhu yin fu hao*, or Symbols for Annotating Sounds, is also known as *Bopomofo* (ㄅ ㄆ ㄇ ㄷ) for the first four syllables of these Chinese phonetic symbols. It is the national phonetic system of Taiwan for teaching the Chinese languages, especially Standard Mandarin. The system uses 37 special symbols to represent the Mandarin sounds: 21 consonants and 16 vowels. Each symbol represents a group of sounds without much ambiguity. (From Wikipedia, the free encyclopedia. http://en.wikipedia.org/wiki/Zhuyin_I)

附　录
汉 语 拼 音 方 案

一　字母表

字母:	Aa	Bb	Cc	Dd	Ee	Ff	Gg
名称:	ㄚ	ㄅㄝ	ㄘㄝ	ㄉㄝ	ㄜ	ㄝㄈ	ㄍㄝ
	Hh	Ii	Jj	Kk	Ll	Mm	Nn
	ㄏㄚ	ㄧ	ㄐㄧㄝ	ㄎㄝ	ㄝㄌ	ㄝㄇ	ㄋㄝ
	Oo	Pp	Qq	Rr	Ss	Tt	
	ㄛ	ㄆㄝ	ㄑㄧㄡ	ㄚㄦ	ㄝㄙ	ㄊㄝ	
	Uu	Vv	Ww	Xx	Yy	Zz	
	ㄨ	ㄪㄝ	ㄨㄚ	ㄒㄧ	ㄧㄚ	ㄗㄝ	

v只用来拼写外来语、少数民族语言和方言。
字母的手写体依照拉丁字母的一般书写习惯。

二　声母表

b	p	m	f	d	t	n	l
ㄅ玻	ㄆ坡	ㄇ摸	ㄈ佛	ㄉ得	ㄊ特	ㄋ讷	ㄌ勒
g	k	h		j	q	x	
ㄍ哥	ㄎ科	ㄏ喝		ㄐ基	ㄑ欺	ㄒ希	
zh	ch	sh	r	z	c	s	
ㄓ知	ㄔ蚩	ㄕ诗	ㄖ日	ㄗ资	ㄘ雌	ㄙ思	

在给汉字注音的时候，为了使拼式简短，zh ch sh 可以省作 ẑ ĉ ŝ。

Source: *Times Advanced Chinese Dictionary* (Times Media Pte Ltd, 1999), p. 1492.

Chairman of the revolutionary committee was a Hainan *ren* [海南人, man who hailed from Hainan province in China]. She, the interpreter, couldn't understand his Mandarin, so I translated his Mandarin to her because I understood his Hainan *qiang diao* [腔调, accent]. The problem for China and the problem for us, is the wide variety of different dialects and accents; (there is a need) to move towards one norm, one standard. Singapore is small and I think we can succeed. China is enormous; I think even in two to three generations, in spite of satellite TV, Internet and so on, they will still be speaking with different accents. The population is huge, each province and town has a different slang and tone — Shanghai is different from Nanjing, Nanjing is different from Beijing and so on.

Language requires that we understand each other. Grammar must always be correct. As in English, you can speak with different accents, but if the grammar is correct, it can be understood. To do all that in Singapore, we have to stick to English and Mandarin. Don't go into dialects, it will ruin the bilingual policy we have. Supposing we had not pushed out dialects, and I had continued speaking Hokkien, today we would be worse off.

Weak in Usage of Words and Phrases

Where I am weak is in the suitability of the phrase. Sometimes I use an unsuitable phrase. For example,

If I were now aged six or seven learning Chinese, it's so much easier.

I used some words which have got a bad meaning — *dui fu* [对付, confront], (as opposed to) *ying fu* [应付, cope with]. You've got to know the difference. When you are not aggressive: it should be *zen yang chu li / ying fu* [怎样处理/应付, how to handle] and not *zen yang dui fu ta* [怎样对付他, how to confront him]. These are not explained in the dictionaries. I need a teacher to point this out to me.

Once I used *qi you ci li* [岂有此理, outrageous], my friend said that's not right, that's telling him off.

These are problems of learning a second language without living the language, without being in an environment where a language comes alive. Otherwise, you could have picked that up from hearing a person scolding the other. I am not sure, perhaps after a while somebody can put in brackets if the word or phrase is criticism or praise, just as transitive verbs and intransitive verbs are indicated in dictionaries. There are very few things you cannot reduce into writing, or symbols to explain connotations, emotive meanings of words, but that has not been done in the current English-Chinese dictionaries. People who compile these dictionaries did not spend time on this aspect of words.

If I were now aged six or seven learning Chinese, it's so much easier. It would be *jian ti zi* [简体字, simplified characters], *pin yin* [拼音, phonetics], *dian nao* [电脑, computers], *ge zhong ge yang de ruan jian* [各种各样的软件, various types of software]. I learnt it the hard way — *fan ti zi* [繁体字,

traditional characters], *zhu yin fu hao* [注音符号] to learn the pronunciation. To use dictionaries, I have to learn *bu shou* (部首, radicals) and *bi hua* [笔划, strokes of the characters].

How Technology Helps

What I do now if I have to make my speech in Mandarin is that I write my speech in English, and send it to MICA [Ministry of Information, Communications and the Arts] to translate it in a literal way. I know that it is stiff, in

Software like these help to make learning Mandarin easier *(archived photograph)*.

written form. So my teacher will change the words accordingly. Then I don't have to follow the script. Having read it two or three times, I just have the text of the speech or some captions in front of me, and I can speak off the cuff. If I have to, I can write my speech in Chinese. New technology enables me to do this.

Today, whenever I don't know the Chinese words, I just type them in English words with my PowerWord dictionary.[12] The (corresponding) Chinese words will appear and I am offered different phrases. You can highlight the words, press "loud speaker", and have Speech Plus read them to you.[13] If the speed is too fast, you make it slightly slower. If I am not sure of the actual tone, I click another icon, its *pin yin* with the tones will be added. I asked Cai Zhili [蔡志礼, Dr Chua Chee Lay] the other day what's "logistics" in Chinese,[14] he

---

[12] PowerWord (金山词霸) is a Chinese and English learning, translation and dictionary software.

[13] Speech Plus (一声通) is a Chinese software that converts text into intelligible voices.

[14] Dr Chua Chee Lay is another Chinese language tutor of MM Lee Kuan Yew.

told me *hou qin* [后勤]. I forgot the character for *qin*, all I need to do is to key in the English word "logistics" using PowerWord, the characters *hou qin* will pop up. As long as the word is in digital form, there is no problem at all. So much frustration avoided.

Now I seldom use my old dictionaries, except when I cannot get the words in digital form. With all these facilities, tools which can be (further) improved, what you must have is the ability to listen and to speak. If you can't understand, that's too bad, nobody can help you. Once you can understand, you can speak the language, you can navigate your way through.

Relate Chinese to English

Teachers should understand that English will be the master language of most students. If they don't relate Chinese to English and teach Chinese as a standalone, the students will lose out. If they have to

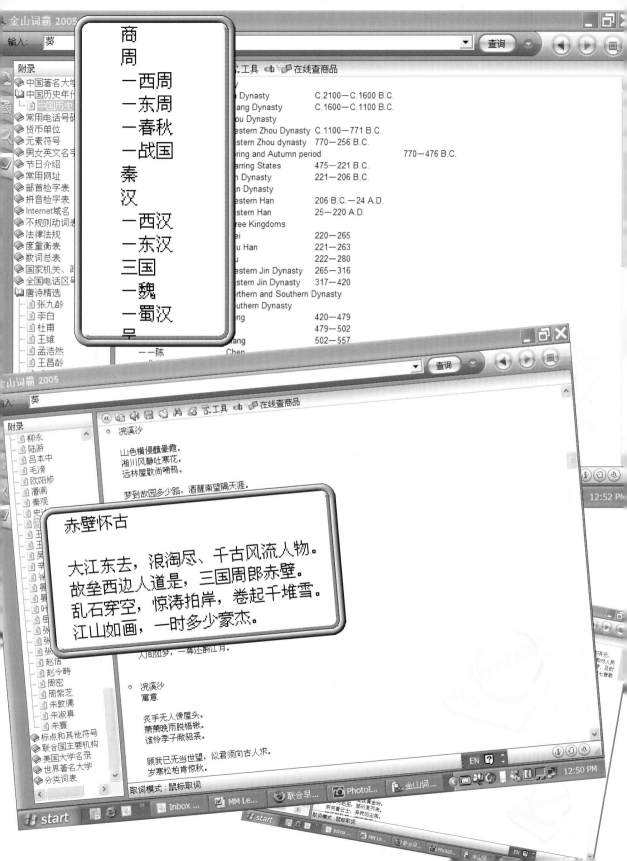

look up a Chinese dictionary, it would a real sweat. At the end of it, they may still be unsure of the meaning. Today with a good English-Chinese dictionary or Chinese-English dictionary, and now with PowerWord, there are so many alternatives given. Once you capture the meaning, it sticks in your mind and if you forget, you go back to the English word, key it into the computer, using the software, you will get the Chinese word. Whereas if you learn Chinese in Chinese and no (correlation with) English, you will not know the corresponding word. Knowing the English word, even if I have forgotten the Chinese word, I can go back to the computer, and get the Chinese equivalent. Learning two languages, with English as the master language, you need to relate Chinese to your English. It is wrong to believe that if you teach Chinese using English, you will weaken the learning of Chinese.

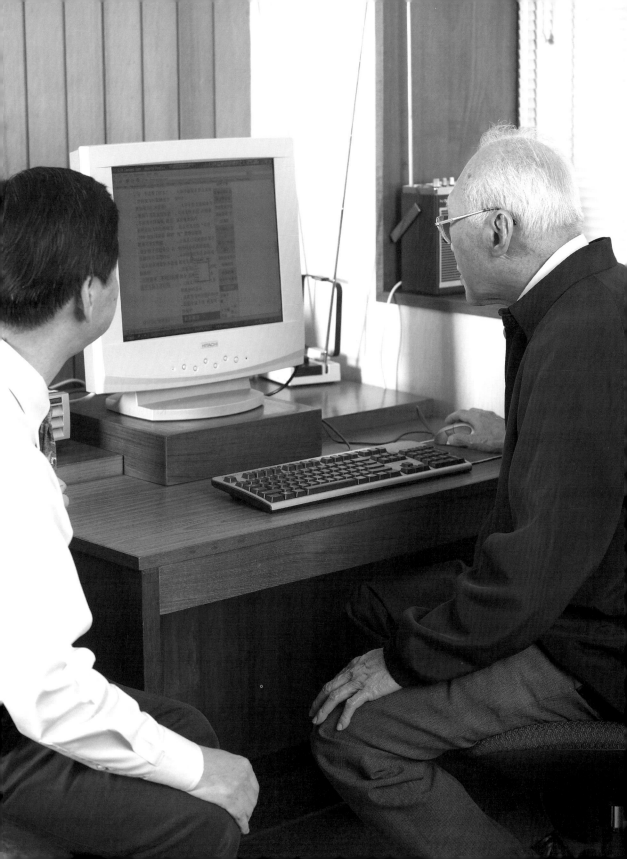

Does this not apply to only the adult learners?

No, no, adults and children alike. What's the master language of my three children? They went to Chinese schools, completely Chinese, English was only (spoken) at home, but English became their master language. If they did not relate Chinese to English, it's lost more easily. It must be related. The interpreters constantly relate Chinese and English words and phrases.

I was speaking at the Central Party School in Beijing just a few years ago. I told the principal that I was speaking off the cuff, no written notes. This was to their *gao ji gan bu* [高级干部, senior officials]. They produced an interpreter who

If you want to learn two languages, you must relate one to the other.

them immediately. (If) you get an untrained person, he thinks about the meaning and then has a free translation in the mind, the translated phrase may not be the same as the one in English. You've got to relate one to the other.

When I learnt Latin, I had to do translations — Latin into English and English into Latin. But our current examinations don't ask that; it's wrong. Chinese into English, English into Chinese — they would reinforce each other. I understand

captured every nuance of my speech. Every tone, every inflection, I watched and listened in amazement. It was total concentration and skill. She was able to relate my English words and phrases to Mandarin and translate

MM Lee feels that if Chinese is not related to English as one learns two languages, it may be lost more easily and this applies to many children too.

because I have been through it and I watched other people. I watched very able ministers, interpreters and I learnt that if you want to learn two languages, you must relate one to the other. Furthermore, if we can, we should teach them grammar, syntax — in English, you say it this way, in Mandarin you say it this other way. Whereas now I am learning not by explanation of the rules but by guessing, which is slow. (On the contrary), at Yale or Harvard, or Chinese language centres in America, their specialists with the help of Chinese professors would have broken down the rules — in English you say it this way, in Mandarin you switch it around and don't say it the same way. So when you have to speak it, it comes out right. Whereas now when I speak Mandarin, I am translating literally from English to Mandarin because I was never taught that way. Had I been taught, I would have known not to say it that way.

? How would you rate your progress in learning Mandarin?

I feel inadequate, not satisfied, because I know it can never be as good as my English. I missed the chance when I was young. Learning (a language) as an adult, you can never have the fluency and the command, because you are always translating in your head. Also, I don't use it so much, therefore, it gets rusty and there's language loss, then I have to revive it. It's a terrible problem because learning it at adult life, it hasn't got the same deep roots in my memory. I notice it with my children because they learnt it [Chinese] from very young. Like my two sons, the first one didn't use it except for casual conversations with his

Both of Lee Kuan Yew's sons went into the army and did not use Mandarin much (*archived photograph from MM Lee*).

soldiers for over 10 or 12 years in the army. Then when he went into politics, he was able to revive it quickly. The other son, he also went into the army, and didn't use Mandarin. Then he went into SingTel.[15] When he went to China, I asked him if he spoke to his host in English or Mandarin, he said in Mandarin, and he had no problem recalling the Chinese words. So, that gave me confirmation that if you learn it young, it comes back quickly. They are like a transistor radio, turn on the volume, the sound comes out. I am like an old valve radio, you switch on, the valve has to be warmed up first. That's the problem.

When I had to do a TV interview in Beijing, this *dui hua* [对话, dialogue], I had to speak in English and only used Mandarin to express myself from time to time, because

---

[15] SingTel, a communications group, is the largest company listed on the Singapore Exchange with a market capitalisation of about S$40 billion (US$24 billion) as of May 2004 (www.singtel.com.sg).

I am like an old valve radio, you switch on, the valve has to be warmed up first.

I was not sure if in Mandarin, I would be able to use the exact words I had wanted. It's a disadvantage but it's the price I pay. I have to pay for not learning the language well.

For me to improve today, I have to live and speak the language for six months or one year in China. If I do so, I think my Mandarin will go up from 50% to 70% or 80%, but my English will go down by 15% or 20% as I won't be using it, and I'll be watching all the Chinese films.

If I keep on using English, then my Mandarin will not improve. If I force myself to use Mandarin every day, for 24 hours a day, I will improve. But there's a price to pay. What is it I need? I don't need that (100% in Mandarin). Before I go to China, I practise Mandarin for three or four lessons. The first few exchanges with the mayor or others, I can do in Mandarin without difficulty. When we start serious discussions, I will be able to understand three-quarters of what is said, then I will answer in English.

It appears that creating this big environment (*da huan jing,* 大环境) conducive to language learning is critical?

Zhou Qinghai [周清海, Professor Chew Cheng Hai] has been teaching me (Chinese) for 30 years now, I meet him once a week. He was determined that his children would continue their Chinese. I told him, "You wait, when they reach A levels, they'll start reading the English papers rather than the Chinese." He didn't believe me. I said, their workload is too much, all their lessons are in English, and they'll have no time (for Chinese). If they have to read newspapers, the English newspaper is so simple, a quick-read. So I asked him recently if his children read the Chinese newspaper now, he said they seldom do so. This

Have the roots to sink into your mind and it will be a lifelong asset.

is a real problem. They are attending to life day by day but at the same time as they have that foundation, if you put them in Taiwan, Shanghai, Guangzhou or Beijing, for six months to one year, they'll catch up. Without that base, its real trouble, a real loss.

When I was in Beijing, I saw our own first or second secretary, a girl, taking notes in Chinese, so I asked her where she was educated. She said a SAP school.[16] I said, "English

---

[16] The Special Assistance Plan (SAP) Schools are government, government-aided or Independent Schools. They were well-established Chinese-medium schools in the past. They offer the Special Course to the top 10% of a cohort which leaves primary school. This is to enable the pupils to be effectively bilingual in both English and Chinese and also inculcate in them traditional values in a Chinese school environment.

as a first language?". She said, "Yes." I said, "But you were able to do it [note-taking] in Chinese." She said only so after six months. So I asked her what she spoke at home, she said it was Mandarin. Coming from a Mandarin-speaking background, even though she took Chinese as a second language, (I believe she must have worked on her Mandarin before she went to Beijing), she could take notes in Chinese as the conversation went on. If you miss that when you are young, then you'll never capture it, it's like me. If I were a computer and I had all the information in my PC, I "control F", I will find what I want. It's different with the brain, "control F", I will only find what I have been using frequently and it is an immediate recall. Therefore, the lesson is: learn it when you are young. So it is important to make the effort. Have the roots to sink into your mind and it will be a lifelong asset. It is something that I have missed which I cannot recover now.

What else can be done?

I once told the English-educated MPs who were learning Mandarin, to have a luncheon club once a week or once a fortnight, to meet and get the Chinese MPs together and speak nothing but Mandarin. Force yourselves and you will keep it up. That was the way I learnt. I had to meet my branch secretaries, my grassroots leaders, I had to speak, but now I don't, so *sheng xiu le* [生锈了, has turned "rusty"]. The effort for this luncheon club was taken up, but only for a while, they had other work.

Nearly all MPs who were Nantah graduates have

Nanyang University was a breeding ground for Mandarin-speaking Singaporeans (*archived photograph*).

retired,[17] except one, Ong Ah Heng. More and more MPs learnt CL2; some still speak good Mandarin but they all speak better English. The language environment is changing, so we must make a special effort. I meet people from the Chinese press, *(Lianhe) Zaobao* [《联合早报》], *Xinmin (Ribao)* [《新明日报》], *(Lianhe) Wanbao*[《联合晚报》], from time to time, and told them to keep one segment of the community alive so that we can regenerate ourselves. If we lose that, to bring it back to life is very difficult.

Like this Yuan Qie Xian [圆切线 or The Tangent],[18] I think it is a good

---

[17] Founded in 1956, Nantah (Nanyang University) was the only Chinese language institution of higher education/learning outside China. It merged with the then University of Singapore in 1980 to form the National University of Singapore.

[18] A Singaporean civil society group which discusses issues mainly in the Chinese language and promotes cross-cultural communication among different segments of society. It publishes a journal, *Tangent*, once in every six months and holds forums regularly to encourage the exchange of ideas.

We'll need this core; it's essential we keep this core.

idea — it's a small group, you will not find many who will do that because this is personal enthusiasm, a personal commitment. Because we have such people, we can regenerate ourselves. If we don't have these people, we are in trouble. Like Malaysia, they gave up English, they went into Malay. The people who know English are already in their fifties, to get (learning English) restarted is a problem. They are now looking for teachers abroad and elsewhere to supplement.

If we lose the transmission from the older generation, who took CL1 [Chinese as a First Language] and whose Chinese is of a high standard, (if) the young generation is not of that standard, we are in trouble. We must keep that [standard of Chinese] up. We can use people from China or Taiwan, but the Chief Editor of the newspapers or TV, the man who sets the line, must be a Singaporean. He must have a Singapore background and have Singapore values

There are probably three to four thousand Singaporeans in China, some of them will have their families there. We have to form an association.

and political sense as his basic position. We'll need this core; it's essential we keep this core. The question is HOW. At the end of the day, it is to get people of higher capability, energy, enthusiasm and ability, to enter these professions or businesses.

There needs to be a programme to keep it [usage of Mandarin] going. It's a question of our education system — what is it that we want to achieve for the majority, what is it that we can achieve for the

top few? I am not sure how many are interested, but the top few are crucial for the cycle to be regenerated. Supposing we lose our journalists, our producers, our educators, how do we restart? Import the teachers? It's not the same. The important thing is to keep the 3 to 5% at the top alive to regenerate. For the vast majority, maybe in the Housing (Development) Board (flats), three or four rooms, they use it [Mandarin] in the hawker centres, shops, restau-

(From left) Lee Choin Nan, editor of the eBook that accompanies this book, showing Lee Kuan Yew contents of the eBook as Chua Chee Lay looks on.

rants and, I hope, at home. They are still buying Chinese newspapers and that's a good sign. But that may change over time, so we have to watch that.

Beyond the top 3 to 5%, there will be a small active group who can reach a higher standard and have more interaction with the Mandarin speaking world. We ought to create situations for them to interact with the people at the top. There are probably three to four thousand Singaporeans in China, some of

them will have their families there. We have to form an association, even those who stop going to China can be members of the alumni. This will keep their hands-on interest up. We must think of ways and means to maintain a lively interest in the language (through interaction) with people, not just with a PC [personal computer]. PC is convenient, it helps, it is a tool, you press the button, it can be repeated several times and you can put it into your mind. But a language must live in people and the people must be our people. Of course we can reinforce it with the Chinese who come to become PRs [permanent residents] or citizens. We form these clubs, when they meet, they will speak in Mandarin. There are several areas the government can help, (including) providing the premises. You meet and gather and keep the language alive through publications, activities, etc.

A language must live in people and the people must be our people.

Does the family not have to play a bigger part then, whether in terms of practising the language or others?

This is one of the biggest dangers we are facing. In this phase, most of our Chinese-educated parents want their children to catch up in their English, so they are speaking English at home to help their children. If they move too fast, too quickly then very few families will be left speaking Mandarin. It will no longer be the home language and very difficult to root the language down. Even though you may not use such a wide vocabulary at home, may not be more than 2000 words — have you eaten, what's your temperature, how did you catch this cold, why are you late — but constant use get their mouths, long ears and minds

Lee Kuan Yew (in tie) listening attentively to his daughter's speech at Nanyang Primary School *(archived photograph from MM Lee)*.

attuned to it. It's like teaching the PC to recognise your voice — you know that's the way people learn and respond to language.

I asked my three children whether I had made a mistake sending them to Chinese schools. They said no emphatically. My sons' children, that's big trouble, because their language environment has changed. Yes, they go to Nanyang Xiao Xue but the students are now speaking to one another in English, and there are only one to two Chinese language lessons a day.[19] So, extra tuition is needed. Therefore we've got to teach the basic. What does it mean? A language must live, it is spoken, it is heard; to read and write is at a secondary stage. Many languages are never

---

[19] Nanyang Xiao Xue, Nanyang Primary School, was founded in 1917 as a Chinese-medium school. It is now one of the SAP primary schools which offers Higher Chinese as early as primary one.

A language must live, it is spoken, it is heard.

written or read, they depend on just oral transmission.

When I was in Suzhou, I went to a town nearby, *Zhou Zhuang* [周庄]. There was a canal, the boat woman could not read but she could recite the Three Represents.[20] The memory is that powerful. By the time they pass primary school, and secondary four, they must be able to listen and to speak. They should be able to read simple words on the wall, on TV or in newspapers. They've got a foundation. They can then pick up and learn more, but if they cannot catch the sound, cannot speak it, that's real trouble. That was my position and that's real effort I had to make. I had to concentrate on the basics first. The others can be built up when necessary.

---

[20] During his inspection tour of China's Guangdong Province in February 2000, Jiang Zemin, then General Secretary of the Communist Party of China, said that the Party has always represented the development trend of advanced productive forces, the orientation of advanced culture and the fundamental interests of the overwhelming majority of the people in China. (http://news.xinhuanet.com/english/20010625/ 422678.htm).

However, when English became the working language, some people struggled to speak the language. Parents spoke halting English — somehow broken — to their kids. Are you worried that the same will happen with the encouragement of a greater usage of Mandarin?

I don't think that's a worry for Mandarin because its pronunciation, its grammar and basic vocabulary are already rooted. Singlish is basically Mandarin in the order of the words. So this order of the words is deeply ingrained in the bulk of the people. I am not worried about debasing Mandarin. I am worried that if you can't speak English properly, and you speak "broken" English to the children, you will confuse them. I believe the community started off as a dialect-speaking community and although dialect is not the same as Mandarin, the grammar is more or less the same.

Are you optimistic that with the rise of China, the bigger environment or *da huan jing* to learn Mandarin is created and more people will be motivated to learn Mandarin?

Yes, it will indeed increase the economic value of Mandarin. At the end of the day, it's (all about) the economic value. But what will happen is that those who are doing business in China or have Chinese partners here, will build up their Mandarin. The rest will be just using it to *mai dong xi* [卖东西, to sell]. You need to learn enough to do business, to get along with the Chinese in China, because China is going to be economically a big player. Not just us, the world will learn Mandarin. Those who want to do business there have to know a lot of Mandarin, and not just know the language, but also know the culture, the politics and the background.

A booming Chinese economy helps increase the economic value of Mandarin. Picture shows Wang Fu Jin (王府井), a popular shopping area in Beijing, China *(archived photograph)*.

At the end of the day, it's all about the economic value.

That's what we must do for maybe 5% of our population so that the people at the top, Trade and Industry Ministry, MFA [Ministry of Foreign Affairs], military and police officers, who have to deal with the Chinese in China would understand Chinese culture as well; know the background of their partners. You cannot know them as well as they know themselves, and you can never know the language as well as they can because it is their language. They are born into the language, the language is their totality, it's everywhere. The accent they put on may be different, so are the idioms, the slang, but the basic language is the same. For us, it [Chinese] is a second language. Even if you make it the first language, it's not the same, you can never equal them. Our value to them is that we understand the world.

Supposing I speak perfect Mandarin, I am of no value to them, but they know that I know a wide

Let's be practical, make ourselves useful first, the value add is English, then Chinese.

spectrum of things which is available to me in the English-speaking world. I meet Americans, British, Europeans and speak English without interpreters. Let's be practical, make ourselves useful first, the value add is English, then Chinese.

For the few of us who have to deal with the Indonesians and Malaysians, do a little Malay. Why do we go for French, German, Japanese? That's only if we are going to study or do business there. This is our environment and for this environment, I'd say the best languages that we can master will be English, Mandarin, Malay. My three children have been exposed to three languages — Mandarin first, English second and then Malay. No problem with that.

Lee Kuan Yew's three children, including his daughter, have been exposed to Mandarin from a young age *(archived photograph from MM Lee)*.

Is there any worry that as more Mainland Chinese know English better, then Singaporeans will lose our edge?

No, no. How many Mainland Chinese can learn English to the level that we can? A very small percentage. They are using Mandarin all the time, they will lose their English. I will give you an example. I used to meet the Taiwanese ministers, the older generation — all Harvard PhDs. In other words, they wrote their theses in English but worked in Taiwan in Mandarin. When I went to Taiwan, I spoke to them in Mandarin, first two days (my Mandarin was) very stiff. At the end of the week, I was more fluent. They came here to meet people from our ministries, first two days their English was halting, at the end of the week they became more fluent. This is a fact of life — the limitations of the brain.

Would you not say that the motivation is the key to the learning of a language?

The motivation for the majority will be economic but if we start early enough, with parents, the motivation is pride in oneself — a sense of identity, consciousness of belonging to a great civilisation; this is where I come from. I'll give you a simple illustration. When I was born, my grandfather consulted his Chinese scholar friend. That's how I got my name. They gave me a piece of paper in Chinese on why he recommended this name, Li Guangyao [李光耀, Lee Kuan Yew]. When it was given to me, I couldn't read Chinese. I felt a deep sense of loss. Later on when I could, I felt a deep sense of accomplishment that I have connected

with the past. That will be true for most people, provided the parents inculcate that into the children. Today, of course, because we are forcing everyone, they are saying, "Enough, I have so much to learn, why am I wasting time with Chinese that I don't need?"

My two boys (my grandsons) stopped learning Chinese at A levels. Now one of my grandsons is at Secondary Four, I asked him if he wanted to continue doing Chinese at A levels, he said, "What for? So much work to do," which I think is a pity. They should not be forced to learn more at that age (about 16), they should keep on using it [Mandarin] so that it sinks deep into the brain. I am not sure academically if this is sound, I have to ask the educationists: Let them carry on without having to learn many more words and phrases, just keep the language living in them and not let it rust away because

> **If we start early enough, with parents, the motivation is pride in oneself — a sense of identity, consciousness of belonging to a great civilisation.**

they are using English at home, playing games in English, watching English TV.

These may change because Chinese TV programmes are going to become equal to what English (American and British) TV can produce. We've already seen the Japanese do that, the Chinese can do the same — it's just a matter of time. So many able people, artists, cartoonists and so on. Given another five, 10, 15 years, that will change. What will not change is that a large amount of energy and time will be spent on using English, but they should keep up their Mandarin so that it is totally rooted. If you keep it up until 18 years old, even if you lose con-nection with it for 10 or 20 years, you can revive it without difficulty. If you give it up when you are 13 or 14, you will find it more difficult to revive subsequently. If you don't have it like me — my first learning of the Chinese characters was in 1942 when I was 19 and I learnt to write, never to speak — that's the problem.

For people who have had some foundation in Chinese but have lost it along the way and now hope to pick it up again, would you have any advice?

If you have the time, or you should make the time, 10 to 15 minutes, read something in Chinese, keep it up. Don't just read passively, silently; read aloud, you must be able to pronounce it correctly. I once went to Harvard for two months in 1968, when I came back to attend a press conference, I could not speak Mandarin easily, the Chinese words were difficult to pull out from my memory. After that when I was travelling for a long time, I would carry a tape-recorder, and I'd play back my Chinese lessons to listen to them. I practise and so I can speak it when I come back. We must know what our limits are and try to keep our Mandarin alive. If you aim for unrealistic standards, you'll be demoralised and turned off.

Do you think that for an adult learner, getting a teacher is essential?

You will need the teacher less, you will need the teacher only to make sure that you are not making mistakes or straying off. But sheer repetition (of a word), to get it into the mind, you don't need teachers, just repeat it. You need a teacher to explain in what other ways the words or phrases can be used, what's the context, the emotional connotation. The PC should be a great help for all the teachers in schools. It'll save them the effort of repeating, they say it once, the students can get it on the PC, the students then go back to listen to it now and again until it sinks in.

Creating an environment conducive to the learning of Mandarin is crucial.

You need to spend the time and effort. You must have the interest.

You need to spend the time and effort. You must have the interest. At the end of the day, it must be a live language. Apart from watching it on the TV or reading the newspapers, you must meet people and talk. Then it is a live language.

Keeping my □ □ □ □ □ □ □ □

Mandarin
Alive

Quotable Quotes

The ultimate test is whether Mandarin is spoken at home between parents and their children.

mother
tongue.

6 Hokkien

It [Hokkien] is not congruent with the written Chinese script. Present-day written Chinese is Mandarin reduced into script. Spoken Hokkien cannot be put into 'bai-hua' [白话, colloquial language]. If Hokkien prevails, then the standard of written Chinese will go down.

23 Dec 1977

Keeping my

Mandarin
Alive

6

Mental Transformers

I used to carry a multi-purpose plug for my tape-recorder when I travel. When I get to a new destination, I had to adjust the plug pins. This will give me a clue on whether or not to change the voltage on the tape-recorder from 240 to 110. **But when I have to switch between English, Mandarin, Hokkien and Malay — never mind Tamil — the mental transformers have even more work to do than the multi-purpose plug.**

10 Feb 1978

6 Deprivation

I say a person who gets deculturalised — and I nearly was, so I know this danger — he loses his self-confidence. You feel a sense of deprivation. For optimum performance, a man must know himself, know the world. He must know where he stands. I may speak the English language better than I speak the Chinese language because I learnt English early in life. But I'll never be an Englishman in a thousand generations and I have not got the Western value system inside me; it's an Eastern value system with the western value system superimposed.

13 Aug 1978

Keeping my

Frequent Usage

Language is heard and spoken long before people learn to write and to read. The more frequently one uses a language, the easier it is to express one's thoughts in it. The younger one learns to speak a language, the more permanently it is remembered.

25 Oct 1981

Mandarin Alive

Self-Esteem

There are several reasons why we want to keep Mandarin. The overriding reason is cultural and the question of self-esteem. You need a sense of your own identity. Next the economic value. In our business with China and Taiwan, you must know the language for your own self-esteem.

Mandarin:
The Chinese Connection, 2000

Mandarin
Alive

6 Keeping Up

I make it a point when I meet my older MPs, the Chinese-educated ones, to talk in Chinese. However out of practice I am, I still speak in Chinese. ... It is one way I have kept my Chinese alive.

Mandarin:
The Chinese Connection, 2000

The more English,

the more

There is no such thing as

100% English,

25 Nov 2004

the less Chinese;

Chinese, the less English.

100% Chinese

Be Realistic

It was unrealistic to set a high standard of achievement in Chinese language. We could not expect to teach Chinese language in bilingual schools at the same level as it had been taught in Chinese schools.

3 Apr 2004

Keeping my

Never Static

Singapore's language climate will never be static. There will always be a backward and forward drift between the English language and the Chinese language. As China becomes a more important economic factor in our lives, the position will shift towards a greater use of the Chinese language.

9 Jul 2004

Mandarin Alive

133

Bilingualism

Bilingualism is difficult, but it is a must for Singapore — for basic reasons of identity, culture and survival. Whatever the standard a student can achieve, he must not be turned off and hate the language. If a student develops an aversion for the mother language, the school has failed.

17 Jul 2004

Keeping my ☐ ☐ ☐ ☐

6 Heartstrings

Because I learned Chinese late in life, and I rediscovered snatches of what I heard when my parents, my grandparents said, "Ah! Yes, that was what they meant." It resonates, pulled at my heartstrings. Would I want to see it lost? Absolutely not!

25 Nov 2004

135

Mandarin Alive

If you have **no master** 6

language,

and you cannot absorb your mathematics, history, science, geography, **either in English or Chinese.**

You are done for.

6 China

China now makes it [Chinese] a language with economic advantages. So we do not have to tell parents, you better do that. When we talked about culture, roots, they were thinking of jobs, security, future. ... My advice to them is: you decide, but do not aim too low. If you aim too low for your child, you may regret it.

25 Nov 2004

Keeping my □ □ □ □ □

Quebec

No country has succeeded in getting its whole population to be bilingual.

It's not been done. I have visited Canada, including Quebec province. Prime Minister Pierre Trudeau tried from 1967 to get all English and French speaking Canadians to learn each other's language. After nearly 40 years, only a top few percent of Canadians are bilingual, English and French speaking. In Quebec, the majority still only speaks French. In the rest of the country, Canadians speak English and few also speak French.

3 May 2005

Mandarin
Alive

Belgium/Mauritius/Luxembourg

It's the same in Belgium between French-speaking (Walloons) and Dutch-speaking (Flemish). So also in Mauritius — once French and then a British colony — where they teach French and English. The people speak Creole, a French pidgin. After independence from the British, they also teach their students their mother tongues, trilingualism, Tamil, Urdu, Chinese, etc. The result is low standards in all languages, seen in their newspapers. It's the same in Luxembourg. They teach French and German, the languages of their two neighbours, while they speak Luxembourgese (their own dialect). Some are now also learning English to serve the international banks in their city. But the level of competence in any language is not high, except for the top few.

3 May 2005

Keeping my

Effective Bilingualism

Effective bilingualism in Singaporeans, English-Chinese, is not more than 3 to 5%; passable bilingualism is another is 20 to 30%. The rest will have average level English, with low level Chinese, or vice-versa (average level Chinese and low level English).

3 May 2005

Mandarin
Alive

Teaching Chinese to Adults

Prof **Chew Cheng Hai**

An Interview with

MM Lee's Chinese Language Tutor

Professor Chew Cheng Hai

11 Mar 2005 | by Chung Poh Leng, Ho Sheo Be

When did you start giving Chinese lessons to MM Lee?

If I remember correctly, it was in 1975.

Have there been any changes to his course curriculum since 1975? For example, in terms of the vocabulary that he picks up, has there been a shift in focus?

MM Lee had mastered a fairly rich Chinese vocabulary already by the 1970s. But he was not quite confident in making sentences with the words he had learnt, nor was he good at joining the sentences to form paragraphs. His listening skill was quite strong, while his ability to speak in Mandarin was relatively weak. However, it should be pointed out that MM Lee has a very solid foundation in pronunciation. I would even say not many among Chinese political leaders in the world could achieve such a high level of accuracy in Mandarin pronunciation.

In the early days, I paid special attention to his sentence structure.

The use of conjunctions, such as "*sui ran* [虽然, although]..., *dan shi* [但是, still?]", "*yu qi* [与其, rather than]..., *bu ru* [不如, would be better?]", and "*yin wei* [因为, because]..., *zai jia shang* [再加上, in addition]..., *suo yi* [所以, therefore]", was what I emphasised. He had in hand words he required to express himself, but he could not complete his sentences, leaving gaps, or should I say, blanks, in between the words. People with whom he conversed had to literally "fill in the blanks" to understand what he meant.

When I first took over the tutorship, I found that though he had acquired a number of Chinese words which he had no problem coming out with, his sentence structure was problematic. Thus, I focused on producing teaching materials pertaining to this area, so as to help him to make structurally sound sentences.

He has once said that learning of a language is like sailing a boat against the current — you either forge ahead or keep falling behind [*ni shui xing zhou, bu jin ze tui*, 逆

水行舟，不进则退]. When I first became his Chinese tutor, he had already memorised many idioms, which he fully understood and was able to use appropriately. My responsibility then was thus two-fold, first, to strengthen his foundation, and second to help him make further progress.

Had the focus then been political and economic terms?

Yes, as a matter of fact, but MM Lee is concerned with different issues at different times. Recently, he is very concerned about the language issue; the tsunami is another. His learning is thus skewed towards these areas. His purpose is to equip himself with sufficient vocabulary to make speeches in the relevant areas. It should be noted that it is not easy for an adult language learner to retain what he has learnt deep in his memory. Therefore, there is the need of ample opportunities for frequent revisions. Although MM Lee is now quite capable of using Mandarin to talk about language issues and culture, politics, economics as well as local customs, he has to frequently revise the words he has already learnt. If he does not have regular revisions, some of the "active" words will gradually turn "passive", and some may even be lost in his memory. When he comes across such words-turned-passive again, he may find them familiar, but it will be difficult for him to use the words to express his thoughts.

MM Lee has once observed that every time after he visited China for a few weeks, his Mandarin would become more fluent, as he would be able to revive the words which have become "passive" in his memory. The implication for a Chinese teacher is, therefore, after you have helped lay the basic foundation for adult language learners, you must continue to help him take stock of what he has learnt and revise at appropriate intervals. Whenever MM Lee doesn't need to make any Mandarin speeches soon after his weekly Chinese class, I will consciously plan for a revision. My teaching materials must be designed in such a way that he is able to revise what he has learnt. Otherwise, I would be wasting his time.

Preparation of revision materials is of course only part of my job. Another important part is to prepare for teaching materials which he may make actual use of in the immediate future. Therefore, when choosing and producing the teaching materials, I must first predict what issues he would need to speak on in, say, three to six months' time. The contents and diction of the teaching materials will have to re-

volve round these issues purposefully. If the teaching materials are not designed in such a way, what I teach and what he would learn will be divorced from what he needs to speak on. To produce appropriate teaching materials for a political leader like MM Lee, a teacher must have a certain degree of political sensitivity.

I would say that it is in the failure to design appropriate revision materials and the inability to foresee what the learner needs to know that lie the reason why some tutors fail to teach well. One day, they select a news report on education, and another day, they use a business report, and then an article of yet a different topic and nature the next time round. Therefore, they do not have a good control of the vocabulary that the language learner needs to pick up; and as a result, it is difficult for the learner to master what he has learnt. Though a language learner may already have some foundation, if the teacher has not prepared appropriate materials to help him revise the words he has learnt, he would easily forget them. If the teacher fails to foresee what the learner will need to speak on and prepare his teaching materials accordingly, the learner will be at a loss when he needs to make a speech, because he has not mastered the required vocabulary. He would have to struggle with the speech, shouldering a huge burden.

You cannot demand that adult language learners learn by heart words that he doesn't need to use in his job or daily life. If, however, the teaching materials contain words a language learner needs, he will be willing to familiarise himself with these words, and with repeated use, he will acquire fluency when talking about related topics, his confidence would in turn be boosted. Some ministers do not have the courage to express themselves even after taking up language lessons. This, I think, is because they have not built up their confidence. If the teaching materials centre on a certain issue on which a minister will need to make a speech in a month's time, he would have sufficient time to make ample practices, and would have mustered more confidence by the time he goes on stage to deliver the speech. He will also be more fluent and will not be reading from the prepared script in *han yu pin yin*. His presentation will be more natural, as he would have memorised the contents of the speech, having spent a long time preparing it.

In other words, a language teacher for a political leader must be aware of major political trends and capable of making educated guesses on what will happen in Singapore and around the world, though admittedly our predictions may not be always be correct. In the case of MM Lee, the cross-Straits relation is always covered in the teaching materials, since it is a recurring issue; you don't know when he would need the relevant vocabulary. So, I will help MM Lee revise the vocabulary on cross-Straits relation every one month or two. The purpose is not to provide him with more information on the topic, but merely to provide him with chances to revise the related vocabulary. The viewpoints of the selected articles should not be skin-deep. It will be better if the articles offer perspectives different from his. But what's most important is that the articles must contain the relevant vocabulary, creating a chance for him to revise what he has learnt.

MM Lee's learning focuses on issues which are of concern to him as a political leader. In other words, we have not had time to touch on literature as well. Ornate language is of no use to him. If we come across a particular historical incident in any of the articles that he is reading, I only have to give a brief explanation of the incident. It's meaningless treating the historical incident as teaching material. When exactly did the incident take place? What dynasty?

Which emperor was then ruling? Such historical facts are not usually of use to him, though it'd be a different story if he is interested to find out.

The same teaching strategy applies also to the case of idioms. Do we have to highlight the origin of an idiom? I would say no if information on the origin does not help him understand the meaning of the idiom better. It will be wasting time and unnecessary.

Of course, I do. After a lesson has ended, I will start preparing the next exercise and teaching materials, based on how he fares in the exercise we have just done. In addition, I predict the issues he may next discuss. If there isn't any major issue he may need to speak on in the immediate future, I will keep using previous teaching materials for his revision.

There are different types, or should I say, domains, of vocabularies in a language. Those who are more proficient in the language will be able to handle many types of vocabularies. However, when it comes to a highly specialised field, even a language expert may not be competent enough to handle the vocabulary in that particular domain. For example, if we talk about economic issues, there will be terms and concepts that I may not fully comprehend, though I may have a basic understanding of the issues. A political leader who is learning a language will not have the competence to master the lexicon of each and every domain. You must build up his confidence in voicing views about issues in the various domains of his concern. You must design the relevant teaching materials accordingly.

Someone once said to me, "I still can't order food at a Chinese restaurant after learning Mandarin." If you learn Mandarin just for the purpose of ordering food in restaurants, that's simple. In such a case, your teaching materials should only consist of the names of different dishes and sampled conversations with waiters and those at the dining table. If an adult learner wants to learn Mandarin only to understand the dining etiquette at a Chinese restaurant and to order food, he has to tell his teacher his objective. The teacher can in turn train him in that area.

For a manager or a CEO who goes to China to play golf with business partners and clients, the teacher has to teach him the words related to the sport. He will invariably need to talk business over the dining table, so the Chinese tutor would also need to teach him the Mandarin terms for the cutlery, the etiquette and what's in the menu, etc. You do not randomly choose an article you like for him to read. Therefore, it requires much to be a successful Chinese teacher. Not anyone who can speak the language well can teach it well.

MM Lee is the only politician I have taught Chinese. For every lesson that lasts 1½ hours, I'll need at least thrice that amount of time to prepare for the teaching materials. After I have chosen the materials based on my hunch, I'd have to amend and re-write the article chosen and pick out the new words. Some experience and understanding of his needs is required to do so. I will also highlight the words which he has previously learnt and which I think he might have forgotten.

For adult learners, is it necessary for them to undergo "one-to-one" learning sessions, i.e., there is only a teacher teaching the learner?

The results for a "one-to-one" session will be better as the teacher will be able to produce teaching materials according to the one learner's needs.

In this connection, I would to like to make a few points on textbook vocabulary. A few years ago, *Lianhe Zaobao* conducted a survey on words and phrases used in the newspaper and the textbooks. I was one of the consultants. Upon completion of the survey, *Zaobao's* personnel-in-charge pointed out in his speech that there were some differences between the vocabulary in *Zaobao* and the words used in the textbooks. He further observed that this might be the reason why our students could not understand *Zaobao* articles. His remarks had reportedly caused a lot of pressure to those who wrote the textbooks. However, I believe it is actually normal for the vocabulary of text-books for primary and secondary school students to be different from the vocabulary found in newspapers articles. Textbook writers and educationists should know that what may interest kids may not interest adults, and what interest adults may not interest kids. Children learning the Chinese language must be able to understand children readers. Many kids are curious about earthworms, but would adults be as interested? No adult uses words such as fox, wolf, lion, tiger and butterfly frequently. If the lexicon meant for children is exactly the same as those for adults, then the textbooks will really be problematic. Therefore, there has to be some differences. The scope of the Chinese vocabulary is very broad, the teacher has to select according to the learning objectives of the learner. The vocabulary for bankers will different from those for other professionals. The words I use when I discuss language issues with language pedagogy researchers will be very different from those I use when trying to obtain pointers from stock traders.

Why have you persisted with teaching MM Lee?

Because he has the passion, and I have seen his improvements; that's most rewarding.

So, how would you rate MM Lee's progress over the years ?

He mainly learns how to speak and read, not how to write. Now, he can practically use Mandarin to discuss any topic. He's very good at listening and speaking, as well as reading. I have seen him progressing all these time. He does not need to write in Chinese. For adult learners of the Chinese language, it is very difficult for them to write. In other words, MM Lee's "passive" vocabulary is very rich. By "passive" vocabulary, I mean those words which one comprehends but does not use when speaking. For any adult language learner, the passive vocabulary will definitely be larger than his active vocabulary. When such a learner hears someone converse in Mandarin, he may not understand one word or two here and there. But he can try to guess and understand the meaning of the word from the context, the paragraphs that appear before or after the word and the situation in which the conversation takes place. After some time, he may be able to understand the meaning of that word, though he may not necessarily know how to use it. Such words are the "passive" words.

What about his Mandarin speeches? Do you give comments on them too?

Yes, I do so when it's time to finalise the draft. I have to help him prepare for the delivery of his speeches.

Were there instances when your views differed from his? Was it difficult to resolve the differences?

Yes, there were, but it would not be difficult to resolve the differences. I would tell him my views. If he can accept them, he would factor them in his speeches. If otherwise, he could at least get to hear views from a different perspective. We have always been frank. There were times when he deleted parts of his speech which I was uncomfortable with. I should believe I am one of his listeners, and I am Chinese-educated. If I don't feel comfortable with a particular point in his speech, then chances are others who are Chinese-educated will also share the same feelings as mine.

Interpersonal relationships are very important. The teacher and the language learner have to show understanding of each other to make the learning process an enjoyable one. I understand his needs, and he knows my expectations; we thus get along well, and that helps make the classes go smoothly. As I help him to learn Chinese, I will have my expectations, and so does he.

Learn as We Teach

Dr Chua Chee Lay

An Interview with

MM Lee's Chinese Language Tutor

Dr Chua Chee Lay

3 Mar 2005 | by Ho Sheo Be, Cheong Chean Chian

Can you tell us under what circumstances were you picked as MM Lee's Chinese language tutor? How you felt when you decided to accept this assignment?

It was by coincidence that I became MM Lee's tutor. MM Lee has taken an interest in the development and application of digital technology, especially that related to the Chinese language, over the past few years. Last August, at the recommendation of Professor Chew Cheng Hai, I went to MM Lee's office to update him on the latest progress in Chinese language IT and also to help him solve some problems concerning the use of Chinese on his computer.

MM Lee asked me many questions on how to make use of technology to make language learning easier, to which I answered matter of factly. After listening intently to my report, his first reaction was that all teachers and children in our schools should get hold of such powerful digital tools to aid their teaching and learning. He even personally chaired a seminar at the Istana for me to present the implications of digital technology on Chinese pedagogy to the three Ministers from the Education Ministry, Members of Parliament with Chinese background and members of the Chinese Language Curriculum and Pedagogy Review Committee.

Not long after, I was notified to take turns with Prof Chew to give Chinese lessons to MM Lee.

To be MM Lee's Chinese tutor is, by anyone's standard, a once-in-a-lifetime opportunity and an enormous challenge as well. Having given Chinese lessons to President SR Nathan, and the then Education Minister and now Defence Minister Teo Chee Hian, I have accumulated valuable knowledge and experience for this new assignment. I also know that I should be frank and honest with MM Lee, as that is the most important value one should possess while facing him.

Can you tell us more about MM Lee's interest in Chinese digital technology and his questions on how to apply it to the learning of languages?

MM Lee is always asking me about the latest development in digital technology, and he is very enthusiastic to know in depth and even personally try out some of the software that could aid language learning. I have introduced to him various quality software such as PowerWord (an English to Chinese,

Chinese to English electronic dictionary), Microsoft's free Chinese package and locally developed and produced programs like Chinese Plus and Speech Plus. I have also introduced to him the well-regarded Google search engine and some important websites.

MM Lee told me that as he is getting on in age and his eyesight is not as good as before, he is finding it very difficult to read if the text on the computer screen is too small. I asked my research partner

Mr Lee Choin Lan to source for a digital magnifying glass which could be used to enlarge images.[*] A week later, a free digital magnifying glass was installed in his computer and MM Lee does not have to squint his eyes on small images on the computer screen anymore.

Although MM Lee is neither a computer researcher nor a teacher, he has brought up many valuable suggestions from the perspective of a language learner. There are many others, including primary school children, who also need to read larger font-sized text. He feels that language learners should be provided with all the conveniences they can get, but they should also put in their utmost to get good results. Many of the dictionaries on MM Lee's table are torn and tattered, which is a testimony to his hard work, but he feels it is very

[*]In order for readers to access this free-of-charge digital magnifying glass, we have included the website address for downloading the software in the Resources section of this book.

tiring and laborious to flip though a dictionary. It is not that he is unwilling to endure this hardship, but that it is not necessary to suffer it. Furthermore, some words cannot be found in the dictionaries, and it is sometimes difficult to differentiate between the component and the radical of a character. Compared to a single hard-copy dictionary, a computer software that brings together a few dictionaries offers ease and speed of checking up a word and is informa-tion-rich. This is the biggest advantage of a digital learning aid.

Can you describe what goes on in a typical lesson for MM Lee?

Our lesson falls every Saturday, starting from around 4.30 pm in the afternoon to about 7 pm in the evening. I gather that MM Lee often looks forward to his lessons and notice that he is very attentive in class. Before every lesson, I will prepare one article as the basic reading material for MM Lee. The article could be either a commentary on current affairs or a news feature from the local Chinese newspapers, or it could be an opinion piece on politics, economics or culture from foreign newspapers. As it is now very convenient to access such information online, most of my teaching materials are taken from the Internet, although they are modified before being used.

Sometimes I will write the teaching materials myself. The advantage is that I can insert some of the words, phrases and sentence structures that MM Lee has recently learnt into the articles, for him to revise them and refresh his memory. I discover that such intentional correlations is rather helpful to language learning.

During a lesson, in addition to the language exercises, MM Lee usually wants me to read aloud one paragraph and then he repeats that paragraph. Besides making sure of the standard pronunciation of each and every word, he is also very particular about grasping the flow and bringing out the essence of a passage while reciting it. I frequently show him where in an article should he stress, pause, raise his voice or drag the end syllable, so as to effect the melodic tone of the Chinese language.

Apart from reading the article and explaining the meaning and usage of various words, we also use an hour of the lesson time to discuss in Mandarin all kinds of topics, including cross-Straits relation, issues on Chinese language teaching and learning, etc.

During every lesson, MM Lee will, without fail, record all of our conversations using a rather archaic tape recorder placed on the large table between the two of us. Each of us has a small microphone pinned on our shirt, as he wants the sound quality of the recording to be good. Whenever he is working out on his bicycle, brushing his teeth, shaving or just resting, he will listen to these recordings over and over again. Even while engaging in leisurely activities, MM Lee is still keeping up with his learning.

Sometimes, while reading the newspapers and there are parts of an article he does not understand, he will underline them and fax to us for explanation. MM Lee is always learning, not just during the weekly lessons. To him, learning is similar to exercising — once a week will not suffice.

Can you share with us some interesting observations during the lessons?

I found it interesting that some of the equipment in MM Lee's office are quite old and have been in use for over 10 years, such as the tape recorder. It seems he is rather fond of antiquated things. He has a stand made of coarse wood and held together by nails, which he likes to use to hold his reading materials. While he has many old equipment, MM Lee is very excited whenever a new edition of a software he is using is available. He cannot wait to un-install the old edition and install the new one to use. He is certainly unique in his value judgement.

What do you gain most from teaching MM Lee Mandarin?

My biggest reward is the opportunity to meet with this world leader every Saturday for two hours, to listen to his unique opinion about world affairs and trivial matters and to discuss and even debate with him on all kinds of issues.

Recently, MM Lee queried about the origin of new Chinese phrases, 哈日 [*ha rì*] and 哈韩 [*ha han*], which often appear in the newspapers. We know these phrases mean craze for Japanese or Korean pop culture, but nobody cares to find out how they come about. I first tried the Power-Word software and then turned to the Internet, but the answers were not to my satisfaction. Later, I checked up the *Xin Hua Xin Ci Yu Ci*

Dian [新华新词语词典, a dictionary of new Chinese phrases] and learnt of their explanation and background. It is through such a process that I am able to explain to him clearly the source of a phrase.

This episode has taught me a valuable lesson: MM Lee is not the only one learning the language. Because of his wisdom, discipline and commitment in learning Mandarin, we begin to take note of things in our daily life that are actually brimming with knowledge for us to discover. Being Chinese tutors to MM Lee has prompted us to be more passionate about life and learning. Our knowledge multiplies along the way.

To be successful in learning a language, the critical factors are enthusiasm and persistence. While you may think that MM Lee is relatively well-equipped in terms of resources, what is more important is his unswerving determination that we should all learn and emulate.

H

哈韩 hā-Hán (craze for S. Korean pop culture) 疯狂崇拜、迷恋和追随韩国的时尚和流行文化。**例**新创力度不够,只好整合老歌,于是《同一首歌》做了一期又一期,也挺受欢迎,因为怀旧是一首永远唱不完的歌。倒是"哈韩"与"哈日"生命力强,乘机再度冲击流行乐坛。(《人民日报》2002 年 1 月 11 日)现在的青少年,有"哈韩一族",他们的热情使得包括服装、发型、饰物、食物乃至生活方式、生活态度在内所有跟韩国有关的东西都迅速升值。(《北京日报》2002 年 9 月 1 日)

😎 *哈日 *韩流 哈狗族 哈哈迷 哈韩族 哈日族 哈衣族 哈哈一族 哈骚时代

哈日 hā-Rì (craze for Japanese pop culture) 疯狂崇拜、迷恋和追随日本的时尚和流行文化。**例**问:现在许多台湾青年疯狂哈日,你作为留日的学生怎么看待这一现象?答:他们只是哈漫画、明星偶像等表象的东西,并不真正了解日本社会。

(《厦门日报》2001 年 9 月 11 日)

📖 "哈日",闽南方言,原义指"被日头毒晒中暑",也可以说"哈着日",意思是"中了日头的毒"。后在台湾青少年中被演绎为一个流行语,用来盲目崇尚、追逐日本的时尚与流行文化,模仿日本时髦少年,崇拜日本演艺明星,追捧日本电视电影、音乐歌曲、图书杂志、动画玩偶、衣着打扮、发型饰物、食品料理等,成为社会上的一种时髦。这些"哈日"的青少年,被冠以略带贬义和轻蔑的称谓——"哈日族"。他们生活环境优裕,受到父母宠爱,消费水平高,自我意识强,追逐时尚,但也不乏攀比和虚荣心,体现了这些青少年些许迷茫,些许激情,些许叛逆和些许青春的躁动。上世纪末与本世纪初,中国大陆也随后出现"哈日"潮流和"哈日族"。"哈日",其实也是善于制造时尚的大众媒体、商人和社会共同打造的一个现象。

😎 *哈韩 哈狗族 哈哈迷 哈韩族 哈日族 哈衣族 哈哈一族 哈骚时代

海归 hǎiguī (returned students) 海外学成归国,多指回国创业。海外学成归国人员称"海归族""海归

派",有时也戏作派"或直接写作"海归"与"海龟"谐音国内对新型人才争夺中国人才的态于是,许多地区从项目,转变到争夺人被称做"海归派"为争夺的焦点。(《年 9 月 28 日)目前次"海归族"主要以下六类人才:……2002 年 2 月 28 日龟"和"土鳖"结合而理人频频被炒,"劳烈的今天,易趣的多没有任何变化。年 3 月 27 日)

😎 海归派 海归海归人士 海归现

海警 hǎijǐng (ma上警察的简称,指边防保卫任务的警上缉毒、反偷渡、缉全、维护领海主权

😎 法警 飞警路警 *水警 *铁警

海撒 hǎisǎ (a kin把骨灰撒入大海的初的"骨灰撒海"说今,北京殡葬处又安

Relating Chinese to English

Dr **Goh Yeng Seng**

An Interview with

MM Lee's Chinese Language Tutor

Dr Goh Yeng Seng

16 Apr 2005 | by Ho Sheo Be

When and under what circumstances did you start to teach MM Lee Chinese?

I obtained my BA in Chinese Language and Literature from the National Taiwan University in 1985 and a PhD in Linguistics from the School of Oriental and African Studies (SOAS), University of London in 1996. I am also specialising in the training of learners of all levels in Chinese language and have been Foreign Minister BG George Yeo's Chinese language tutor for 15 years.

With the recommendation of Professor Chew Cheng Hai and the support of BG Yeo, I met up with the then Senior Minister Lee Kuan Yew in April 2001. From June that year, I was the "relief teacher" of MM Lee when Prof Chew was out of town. After about a year, MM Lee proposed taking time off his hectic schedules to have weekly lessons with me. However, my hands are full with teaching and administrative work in the National Institute of Education, as well as teaching other government leaders Chinese. I began to give MM Lee monthly lessons after some adjustment.

What's your focus during the lessons?

Basically, there are two major teaching methods: free discussions and self-developed teaching materials. For the former, the content is wide-ranging, and includes politics, economics, language and social issues pertaining to China, Taiwan, Hong Kong and Singapore.

The subject of discussion hinges on what's the topical issue.

As for self-developed teaching materials, I select those which are in line with MM Lee's learning objectives and personal interests, and are topical issues that warrant much press coverage. Some examples are the 9-11 incident, China's entry into WTO [World Trade Organisation] and the SARS epidemic. To ensure a rich variety, I select reading materials from various sources: China's *Nan Fang Zhou Mo* [南方周末, translated as *Southern Weekend*], Taiwan's *Tian Xia* [天下 or *Commonwealth Magazine*], Hong Kong's *Yazhou Zhoukan* [亚洲周刊] and Singapore's *Lianhe Zaobao* [联合早报], just to name a few. They are newspaper and magazine reports, personal publications, electronic letters, official releases and online forum letters. The authors are from different background: scholars, diplomats, journalists, government officials who disseminate official releases and the masses. My teaching materials are taken from various sources to provide multiple perspectives, including opposing views on controversial issues in Singapore.

In his interview, MM Lee mentioned the acquisition of passive and active vocabulary, how do you help him in acquiring these?

Active vocabulary can be likened to productive vocabulary which is of practical usage in terms of speech and writing, while passive vocabulary is receptive vocabulary which has to do with listening and reading. Generally speaking, a person's command of the passive vocabulary is twice that of the active vocabulary.

In the free discussions mentioned above, which are to improve MM Lee's oral skills, although the focus is on fluent oral usage, I would correct his usage of the Chinese words and phrases when necessary, without affecting his thread of thought. When he wants to relate a Chinese word to English, I will also help him along. If he does not understand the meaning of a certain Chinese word that I use, he would request that I provide its English equivalent. This helps MM Lee in his acquisition of active (reproductive) vocabulary.

As the self-developed teaching materials are mainly to improve MM Lee's receptive skills in reading, as well as to widen the scope of his passive vocabulary, the content and sources of these materials is wide-ranging, and the language style rich. At the same time, each reading material carries a glossary of new words which includes the pronunciation and the English explanation of the words. In addition, each of the materials includes exercises such as filling in the blanks, pairing words and making sentences, to strengthen his command of the active vocabulary.

What strikes you most in the course of teaching MM Lee Chinese and how has that influenced you?

MM Lee is very open-minded. Even though our views on various topics may differ, I can have rational debates with him freely. This has not only helped in upgrading my expertise in the linguistics, it has widened my research interest and horizon. His sharp political wisdom and comprehensive world views, particularly those relating to cross-Straits relations, the rise of China, regional integration, international relations and Singapore's politics and economics, are constant sources of inspiration. Such influence has indeed prompted me to decide to spend six months at the Fairbank Centre for East Asian Research of Harvard University to research on a topic entitled, "Who are We? The China Complex of Chinese in Singapore: Reactions to the Taiwan Visit of Former Singapore Deputy Prime Minister Lee Hsien Loong" delivered at the Centre on 19 May 2005.

Rather than saying that I am teaching MM Lee Chinese, it is better to put it as a mutually beneficial process which we both learn and gain. In the process of teaching MM Lee Chinese, I have continued to ponder about issues related to the Chinese-English bilingual pedagogy. With his support, I provided academic advice to the Ministry of Education (MOE) for a three-year pilot project on "Bilingual Approach to the Teaching of Chinese Language" in four primary schools, to explore the feasibility of using English (first language or L1) to help students learn Chinese (second language or L2), particularly those who come from English-speaking homes.

MM Lee's experience in learning Chinese is of reference value particularly to those who took CL2. As mentioned, all self-developed teaching materials use English to explain the meaning of new words. Such a learning method, which employs English and electronic dictionaries in two languages as supplementary tools, is very effective in helping MM Lee to comprehend and remember the Chinese vocabulary. Based on his personal experience in learning Mandarin, MM Lee is supportive of the transitional bilingual pedagogy directed mainly at those who come from English-speaking families. This bilingual teaching approach allows the usage of English as a supplementary language medium of instruction at the beginning. This is subsequently replaced with Chinese as the learner progresses, thus achieving the learning objective.

When this pilot project was first launched, reactions of Singapore's Chinese and English speaking communities were on opposite ends. The former objected to it vehemently, while the latter embraced it readily. The Chinese and English newspapers had a field-day covering such tussles and debates.

I took the opportunity of my stint as a visiting scholar in Harvard to visit several educational institutions (universities and schools) in Eastern US in the field of teaching Chinese as a foreign language. I observed that in the US where English is the dominant language, using English as a supplementary tool in learning Mandarin has been prevalent for several years. Singapore can certainly take a leaf from some of these teaching methods.

However, as the number of Chinese Americans who learn Chinese in the universities multiplies in recent years, Chinese language educators in North America face a new challenge in tailoring the lessons to suit the needs of students with varying levels of competence. They found out that lumping those with some basic Chinese oral skills and those without did not do either party any good. Thus, several universities adopted the "double-track" for beginners. Coincidentally, Chinese schools are also facing a similar problem as the number of Chinese children who are adopted by American and European families increased. These children's language background is very different from Chinese-Americans who speak Mandarin at home. Thus, the Chinese schools have also adopted the "double-track" system , one using only Chinese and the other using English as a supplementary tool for English-speaking children.

Singapore may consider adopting such "double-track" systems to cater to the different needs of those who speak Mandarin and English at home. Otherwise, both parties would not benefit.

Would you say that MM Lee's learning experience can be applied to other adult language learners as well and how?

MM Lee's Chinese classes concentrate on developing the skills in listening, reading and speech; for him, writing is a matter of translating English into Chinese. This learning strategy is particularly useful for professionals from Singapore's public and private organisations who are keen to venture into China. This is so because, if Singaporeans are capable of speaking Mandarin in their conversations with the Chinese in China, the gap between the two parties can be bridged. While equipping oneself with listening and oral skills is fundamental, basic skills in reading Chinese is also essential as anyone with dealings in China would have to read primary materials written in Chinese.

It is most difficult to acquire writing skills. Singaporean professionals may write their drafts in English and then seek professional help in translating them into Chinese. This is then followed by amendments and adaptations to suit their needs. MM Lee, whose first language is English, as well as other American or British experts on China matters, have indeed been using such a method in their interactions with their counterparts in China and it has been working rather well. Such language learning strategy is thus particularly beneficial to adults who learnt Chinese as a second language.

Learning Materials

对话

甲：最近，苏门答腊岛北部的居民惨遭海啸蹂躏，
灾情严重，我们应该伸出援手，帮他们一把，
绝不能隔岸观火(1)啊！
gé àn guān huǒ

乙：嗯，老兄，你这么说就不对了。

甲：难道说，帮助邻国受苦受难(2)的灾民也有错
shòu kǔ shòu nàn
吗？如果不是苏门答腊岛为我国挡住(3)这一场
dǎng
排山倒海(4)而来的海啸，恐怕我们也难逃这一
场世纪(5)浩劫(6)！
hào jié

乙：我不是这个意思。人非草木(7)，岂有见死不救
之理(8)。况且(9)，有能力帮助别人是一种福
kuàng qiě
气。我说你说错了，指的是你的成语用错了。

甲：哦？请您多多指教。

乙：你用"隔岸观火"就不对了。试想想，大海啸掀起的是滔天巨浪，造成的是泛滥成灾(10)。都是大量水带来的祸害。哪里来的火呢？

甲：说的也有道理。不过，我现在只是用来比喻罢了！难道这也不行吗？

乙：当然不行。语文的应用，讲究的就是精准(11)得体(12)，您用火灾来比喻水灾，怎么说得过去呢？

甲：那照您说，该用什么成语比较适合呢？总不能改为"隔岸观水"吧？

乙：那当然不行，成语怎么能要改就改，想怎么改就怎么改。如果大家都随心所欲(13)地胡乱改变成语，岂不是天下大乱(14)？成语就"成"不了"语"了！

话说回来，依我看，我们只要用"看见邻国有

难，我们不能袖手旁观(15)"，就行了。

甲：哗！您说得很有道理。不但见解精辟，而且还

能以理服人(16)，小弟真是佩服(17)！佩服！

乙：哪里，哪里。您过奖(18)了。其实有空的时候，

大家不妨(19)多切磋(20)切磋，语文自然就会

进步。

1. 隔岸观火：
gé àn guān huǒ
Watch a fire from the opposite side of the river.
隔着河水在对岸看火灾。
比喻在一个安全的地点看着别人遭受灾难。

2. 受苦受难：
shòu kǔ shòu nàn
suffering 遭受许多痛苦

3. 挡住：
dǎng zhù
to block; to stop 阻止

4. 排山倒海：
　　pái shān dǎo hǎi

Topple the mountains and overturn the seas.

把山推开，把海翻过来。

形容声势浩大，来势凶猛。

排：arrange 安排；eject/exclude 排除； line 一排排；rank 等级

5. 世纪：
　　shì jì

Century 一百年

世：age 时代；era 纪元；generation 一代；life/lifetime 一生/寿命；world 世界

纪：age 年代；epoch 时代；period 时期；record 记录；discipline 纪律

6. 浩劫：
　　hào jié

great calamity; catastrophe 巨大的灾难

浩：vast; grand; great

浩浩荡荡：vast and mighty

劫：disaster 灾难；plunder; rob 抢劫

7. 人非草木：
　　rén fēi cǎo mù

We are human with affection and not plants with no feeling.

人是有血、有肉、有情、有义的，并不是无情无义的植物。

8. 岂 有 见 死 不 救 之 理：
   qǐ yǒu jiàn sǐ bù jiù zhī lǐ

   How can we see someone dying and not give a helping hand?
   哪有眼睁睁地看着有人快死了，我们却不愿意救他的道
   理？
   (白话)　哪有……………………的道理？
   (文绉绉) 岂有……………………的道理？
   岂有此理：哪有这样的道理？

9. 况 且：
   kuàng qiě

   moreover; besides; in addition　表示"更进一层"；更何况。

10. 泛 滥 成 灾：
    fàn làn chéng zāi

    disaster caused by flooding waters; be swamped by; run rampant
    大量的水流出来，造成非常严重的水灾。
    喻指过多的东西，会成祸害，也指不良的思想、言行广为
    流传，危害很大。

11. 精 准：
    jīng zhǔn

    accurate　非常准确；非常正确。

12. 得 体：
    dé tǐ

    appropriate　言行恰到好处。

13. 随 心 所 欲：
suí xīn suǒ yù

have one's own way; do as one likes

完全按照自己的意愿去做事。

随心：follow the heart

欲：desire; wish for

14. 天 下 大 乱：
tiān xià dà luàn

the whole world is in confusion; chaos; turmoil

秩序严重破坏；大骚乱

天下：under the sun (sky)

15. 袖 手 旁 观：
xiù shǒu páng guān

look on (stand by) with folded arms

在一旁看，不过问，也不帮忙

袖：sleeve

16. 以 理 服 人：
yǐ lǐ fú rén

persuade through reasoning; convince somebody by sound argument

用道理使人信服

17. 佩 服：
pèi fú

admire; have admiration for 钦佩；信服

18. 过 奖：
guò jiǎng

over praise; give someone too much credit 过分的赞扬

19. **不 妨**:
　　bù　fāng

might as well 最好还是

20. **切 磋**:
　　qiē　cuō

learn from each other by exchanging views; compare notes

比喻学问和技能等方面，相互研讨勉励

磋商：consult; advise with

仔细商量；研究

新加坡狮有个<ruby>性<rt>gè xìng</rt></ruby>(1)！

取自《联合早报》电子版

　　代表新加坡多元文化特色及刚<ruby>强<rt>gāng qiáng</rt></ruby>(2)勇<ruby>猛<rt>yǒng měng</rt></ruby>(3)精神的本地舞狮<ruby>家族<rt>jiā zú</rt></ruby>(4)新成员"新加坡狮"，昨晚在裕廊东体育场内，近万名观众的欢呼声中<ruby>诞生<rt>dàn shēng</rt></ruby>(5)。

　　穿上红色传统<ruby>唐装<rt>táng zhuāng</rt></ruby>(6)的李显龙总理及其他嘉宾，为十头新加坡狮主持<ruby>点睛<rt>diǎn jīng</rt></ruby>仪式(7)。

　　李总理对新加坡狮的<ruby>特征<rt>tè zhēng</rt></ruby>(8)，作了很<ruby>生动<rt>shēng dòng</rt></ruby>(9)的<ruby>形容<rt>xíng róng</rt></ruby>(10)。

　　"这头具有新加坡特征的狮子，<ruby>样貌<rt>yàng mào</rt></ruby>(11)和传统的舞狮很不一样，它的<ruby>胡子<rt>hú zi</rt></ruby>(12)看起来比较长，牙齿也比较尖，但是<ruby>表情<rt>biǎo qíng</rt></ruby>(13)还是相当<ruby>温驯<rt>wēn xùn</rt></ruby>(14)的。"

他说："带动(15) 舞狮的有华族的锣鼓(16)、马来族的羊皮鼓[kompang](17) 和印度族的鼓乐 (18)，象征(19) 着新加坡的多元种族社会。我希望它能使国人的认同感(20) 更加浓厚(21)，加深我们对国家的感情。"

以代表国旗的红白两色设计(22) 的新加坡狮，是以铿锵(23) 的华族锣鼓带动(24) 舞狮节奏(25)，舞步(26) 即扎实(27) 又灵活多变(28)，更以华巫印族的传统舞蹈配合(29)，散发多元文化的色彩(30)。

李总理受访时说，舞狮是新加坡华族的传统文化，而且也深入人心(31)。

"不只华族喜欢舞狮，马来族和印度族同胞日子久了，也觉得舞狮是他们共有的文化的一部分。"

因此，他希望新加坡狮不但能加深人民对国家的感情，也能获得国人的认同，成为本国文化的一部分。

gè xìng
1. 个性：
character; individuality; personality

gāng qiáng
2. 刚　强：
strong; staunch; firm
意志性格等坚强、不在恶势力前低头、不畏艰难。

yǒng měng
3. 勇　猛：
be full of valour and vigour; be bold and powerful　英勇骠悍

jiā　zú
4. 家　族：
clan; family

dàn shēng
5. 诞　生：
be born; come into being
指人出生，也用于比喻新事物的出现

6. 唐　装：
tángzhuāng

dress or clothing of Tang dynasty 唐代的服饰装束。

7. 点　睛：
diǎn jīng

the act of adding pupils to a dragon 来自成语故事《画龙点睛》
Based on this fairy tale, the last touch added to a drawing is said to be
the act of adding pupils to a dragon, that is to say, the last touch in a
masterpiece is the most important part of a drawing, or any other
important business.

8. 特　征：
tè zhēng

characteristic; distinguishing feature 指异于他事物的特点

9. 生　动：
shēng dòng

vivid; lively; dramatic 具有活力能使人感动的

10. 形　容：
xíng róng

describe 描述

11. 样　貌：
yàng mào

appearance; shape 外观、形状

12. 胡　子：
hú zi

beard 胡须

胡：

1. black 黑

2. outrageously; recklessly

任意乱来

例：胡说；胡闹；胡搞

biǎo qíng
13. 表 情：

facial expression 表达在面部或姿态上的思想感情

wēn xùn
14. 温 驯：

gentle; facile; kindly; mild; peaceable; soft 温和

驯服：tame and docile 温和顺从

dài dòng
15. 带 动：

drive; bring about; spur on; set the pace

luó gǔ
16. 锣 鼓：

gong and drum 铜锣与大鼓

yáng pí gǔ
17. 羊 皮 鼓

kompang

羊皮 sheep skin

gǔ yuè
18. 鼓 乐：

strains of music accompanied by drumbeats

19. 象 征：
xiàng zhēng

symbolise; emblematise; indicate; represent; signify; stand for; symbol

20. 认 同 感：sense of identification
rèn tóng gǎn

归 属 感：sense of belonging
guī shǔ gǎn

21. 浓 厚：dense
nóng hòu

22. 设 计：design
shè jì

23. 铿 锵：
kēng qiāng

clangorous; sonorous

形容乐器声音响亮节奏分明,也用来形容诗词文曲声调响亮,节奏明快。

24. 节 奏：
jié zòu

rhythm 音乐中交替出现的有规律的强弱、长短的现象

25. 舞 步：dancing steps
wǔ bù

26. 扎 实：well-knit
zhā shi

扎：prick; plunge into; get into

实：solid and truthful

27. 灵活多变：
（líng huó duō biàn）

    灵活：nimble; agile; quick; clever

    快捷；不死板

    多变：changeable; varied 易变的

28. 配合：
（pèi hé）

coordinate; cooperate

为共同任务分工合作，协调一致地行动

配合得宜；配合作战

29. 散发：
（sàn fā）

emanate

30. 色彩：hue; colouration; tinge
（sè cǎi）

31. 深入人心：
（shēn rù rén xīn）

strike root in the hearts of the people;

be deeply rooted among the people;

find its way deep into the people's heart

指思想、理论、学说、主张等广为人们所理解和接受。

Adding Pupils to a Dragon

Once a famous artist Zhang Seng You drew four dragons on the walls of An Le Temple, Jin Ling, but he left the pupils of the dragons unfinished. Someone asked him the reason of the omission. In answer, he said that if he put the pupils therein the dragons would become alive and fly away. The questioner did not believe it and requested him to complete the work. The artist nodded assent. But as soon as the two dots were drawn, all of a sudden, there were thunder and lightning and the dragon became alive and instantly flew away, while the other three without pupils still remained there.

Based on this fairy tale, the last touch added to a drawing is said to be the act of adding pupils to a dragon, that is to say, the last touch in a masterpiece is the most important part of a drawing, or any other important business.

画龙点睛

有一次，著名艺术家张僧<ruby>繇<rt>yáo</rt></ruby>在<ruby>金陵<rt>jīn líng</rt></ruby>安乐寺墙壁上画了四条龙，故意没有把眼睛画上。有人问他不画眼睛的道理，他说："我如果把眼睛画上，那龙就要飞走了。"问他的人不相信，要求他把龙画完整。这位艺术家答应了。可是当一条龙的眼睛画上后，突然雷电交加，那龙真的活了，立刻向天上飞去，其余没有眼睛的龙，仍留在墙上。

根据这个神话，后人就把绘画上最后的重要一笔，称为"画龙点睛"，就是说，最后一部分工作是工作中最精彩，最重要的一部分。

jié lù　　　　　gǎi xiě
节录(1)并改 写自：《中国东方早报》，
2005年1月5日

　　近年来，不仅(2) 新加坡市民对中文热情 高 涨
(3)，而且新加坡政府在加强语言 政 策(4)，和推广中
文普及(5) 方面也不遗余力(6)。

　　新加坡人对待中文的态度可说是有了很大的变
化。根据对新加坡全国四百名中学生的调 查(7)，有
百分之八十三的华人学生认为，母语是汉语；百分
之九十七的人为自已会讲汉语，而感到骄傲(8)；百
分之九十五的被调查者认为，华人应该学习汉语，
其中百分之三十二的人认为，汉语应该学习到大学
程度。此外，有四分之三的学生家长鼓励子女学好
汉语。

包括前总理李光耀在内的社会显要(9)人士，也为中文教育推波助澜(10)。李光耀资政在不同场合(11)指出，4岁到12岁是儿童学习过程中，非常重要的阶段(12)。他希望更多的父母，能让孩子在幼儿园和上小学期间，就接触(13)汉语，以奠定(14)良好的语言基础(15)。

在新加坡，英语、华语、马来语和淡米尔语为官方语言。在教学、商业、出版、公务等方面，使用各民族语言文字都是合法(16)的。英语列为(17)行政语言(18)，成为各民族共通(19)的语言。大部分新加坡人，尤其是年轻一代，都能用流利的英语交谈。此外，新加坡人大多通晓(20)本民族的母语。

几十年来，政治力量影响着这个国家的语言方向，世局(21)变换(22)，国际大势力(23)洗牌(24)角力(25)，都不同程度地影响，中文在新加坡的流通(26)。

在上世纪后期(27)，为了安身立命(28)，新加坡人选择了英语。但是，在新加坡华人的内心中，仍然保留着讲汉语的愿望(29)。

1979年，新加坡前总理李光耀发起"讲华语运动"，目的是要鼓励新加坡华族在政治、社会及商业阶层(30)上，多使用华语，以努力争取华语在英语主导(31)的环境下，还能继续生存的空间(32)。否则，华语将会成为让人瞧不起的"厨房(33)里的语言"。我们可以把"讲华语运动"的发展过程，看作是新加坡华语命运(34)的一个历史缩影(35)。

新加坡华语包含了一种特殊(36)的"政治价值"(37)，它维系(38)着新加坡华人对中华语言和文化的深厚情感(39)。今天，随着全球华语升温(40)，以及中国的和平崛起(41)，给中文在新加坡的继续生存，创造了一个更广阔和更有利的外在环境。

　　除了推广的华语普及教育之外，新加坡政府也大力推行华文精英(42)教育。一些非常优秀(43)的华族子弟，除了学习汉语以外，中国的政治、经济、历史、文化等等课题，都是他们需要深入学习的。借用李光耀资政的话来说，普及华文固然(44)重要，同时更要培养出精通双语和双文化的"中国通"(45)。

1. 节录：
　　extract；excerpt 摘录；选录
　　例：从这本书中节录出几段文字。

2. 不仅(2)：
　　not only
　　不仅……而且 Not only...but also
　　例：这里的食物不仅好吃，而且很便宜。

3. <ruby>热<rt>rè</rt></ruby> <ruby>情<rt>qíng</rt></ruby> <ruby>高<rt>gāo</rt></ruby> <ruby>涨<rt>zhǎng</rt></ruby>：

   enthusiasm; fervent 具有强烈感情、激情或热心。

   例：观赏足球的人们热情高涨。

4. <ruby>语<rt>yǔ</rt></ruby> <ruby>言<rt>yán</rt></ruby> <ruby>政<rt>zhèng</rt></ruby> <ruby>策<rt>cè</rt></ruby>：

   language policy

5. <ruby>普<rt>pǔ</rt></ruby> <ruby>及<rt>jí</rt></ruby>：

   gain ground; popularisation; prevalence

   例：普及教育，对人人有利。

6. <ruby>不<rt>bù</rt></ruby> <ruby>遗<rt>yí</rt></ruby> <ruby>余<rt>yú</rt></ruby> <ruby>力<rt>lì</rt></ruby>：

   do everything in one's power; do one's best (utmost);

   spare no effort (pain)

   把所有的力量都用出来，一点都不保留，形容尽心尽力。

   例：校长不遗余力地把学校办好。

7. <ruby>调<rt>diào</rt></ruby> <ruby>查<rt>chá</rt></ruby>：

   survey

   例：经过详细的调查之后，真相终于水落石出。

8. <ruby>骄<rt>jiāo</rt></ruby> <ruby>傲<rt>ào</rt></ruby>：

   proud of

   例：新加坡的成就，是我们的骄傲。

9. 显要：
xiǎn yào

influential figure; powerful and influential

10. 推波助澜：
tuī bō zhù lán

add fuel (oil) to the fire; set the heather on fire; make a stormy sea
stormier

从旁鼓励，以增加声威和力量

例：如果不是媒体推波助澜，大事宣传，我们无法筹到那
么多善款。

11. 场合：
chǎng hé

situation; occasion; context

例：不同的场合有不同的气氛。

12. 阶段：
jiē duàn

stage; phase; period

例：这个工程分三个阶段进行。

13. 接触：
jiē chù

contact; meet

例：各族之间应该多接触，多了解他族的文化习俗。

14. 奠定：
diàn dìng

establish; settle

例：他经过多年的努力，终于奠定了事业成功的基石。

15. 基 础：
_{jī　chǔ}

foundation; base; basis; cornerstone; ground-work

例：新加坡有良好的基础设施。

16. 合 法：
_{hé　fǎ}

legal; lawful; legitimate

例：惟有依据法律行事，才算合法。

17. 列 为：
_{liè　wéi}

listed as

例：这房子被列为古迹保留下来。

18. 行 政 语 言：
_{xíng　zhèng yǔ yán}

language for administration

19. 共 通：
_{gòng　tōng}

applicable to both or all; common

例：华语是华族的共同语。

20. 通 晓：
_{tōng xiǎo}

thoroughly understand; be well versed in; be proficient in

完全掌握，透彻地了解

例：通晓多种语言对我们好处多。

jī　chǔ
15. 基 础：

foundation; base; basis; cornerstone; ground-work

例：新加坡有良好的基础设施。

hé　fǎ
16. 合 法：

legal; lawful; legitimate

例：惟有依据法律行事，才算合法。

liè　wéi
17. 列 为：

listed as

例：这房子被列为古迹保留下来。

xíng　zhèng　yǔ　yán
18. 行 政 语 言：

language for administration

gòng　tōng
19. 共 通：

applicable to both or all; common

例：华语是华族的共同语。

tōng　xiǎo
20. 通 晓：

thoroughly understand; be well versed in; be proficient in

完全掌握，透彻地了解

例：通晓多种语言对我们好处多。

21. 世局:
shì jú

current world situation

例：世局变换莫测，领导必须随机应变。

22. 变换:
biàn huàn

switch; transform

23. 大势力:
dà shì lì

force; influence

24. 洗牌:
xǐ pái

shuffle

例：每赌一局，都要洗一次牌。

例：最近公司的人事好像又在洗牌，许多主管又大调动。

25. 角力:
jué lì

wrestle; strength trial

例：经过角力之后，终于分出胜负。

26. 流通:
liú tōng

circulation

例：这种货币已经不再流通了。

27. 后期:
hòu qī

later stage 某一时期的后一阶段

例：我在五十年代后期出世。

ān shēn lì mìng
28. 安 身 立 命：

settle down and get on with one's pursuit

例：只要国泰民安，大家就能安身立命，为将来的好日子
努力工作。

yuàn wàng
29. 愿 望：

hope

例：新年新愿望。

jiē céng
30. 阶 层：

class

例：社会上各个阶层的人士都参加义工活动。

zhǔ dǎo
31. 主 导：

leading; dominant; guiding 推动全局发展

例：一个政策的成功与否，除了政府的主导，民间的配合
也很重要。

shēng cún kōng jiān
32. 生 存 空 间：

space for living

例：1965年的新加坡，几乎没有生存的空间。

chú fáng
33. 厨 房：

kitchen

例：她上得了厅堂，进得了厨房。

34. 命运：
mìng yùn

fate; destiny

例：努力可以改变命运。

35. 历史缩影：
lì shǐ suō yǐng

historical miniature (epitome)

例：牛车水是早期新加坡华人社会的缩影。

36. 特殊：
tè shū

special; exceptional 和普通的不一样。

37. 政治价值：
zhèng zhì jià zhí

political value

38. 维系：
wéi xì

hold together; maintain 维持和联系

系：band; rope; cord 绑住物品的带、绳

例：三年前，我和他失去联系。

39. 情感：
qíng gǎn

emotion; feeling

40. 升温：
shēng wēn

warming up 温度升高

例：我们应该注意环保，免得地球逐渐升温。

41. 崛起：
    jué qǐ

    spring; rise 兴起
    例：新加坡崛起成为亚洲四小龙。

42. 精英：
    jīng yīng

    outstanding person; elite
    例：这所学校培养了许多政坛精英。

43. 优秀：
    yōu xiù

    excellent; outstanding 出色，非常好。
    例：他是国家队里最优秀的球员。

44. 固然：
    gù rán

    no doubt; of course; certainly
    例：工作固然重要，但是家庭也不可以不照顾。

45. 中国通：
    zhōng guó tōng

    Chinese expert; China watcher
    例：新加坡计划培养许多中国通。

书到用时方恨少

作者公孙笑

取自《联合早报》，2005年3月27日

　　中国总理温家宝在中外记者会上，经常旁 征 博 ^{páng zhēng bó} 引(1) 诸子百家(2) 作品，"以诗言志"(3)，却因此而使不少在座记者感叹(4) 书到 用时 方 恨 少(5)，事后忙于查询(6) 它们的出处(7) 和寓意(8)。

　　我国国务资政吴作栋最近在"新加坡季在伦敦"的开幕仪式上，则引用(9) 英国大文豪莎士比亚的名言，说明新加坡必须不断改革创新。

　　"新加坡季"将来推广到中国各大城市时，部长们会不会也入乡 随俗(10)，用华语朗诵几段隽 永(11) 的中国古诗词？或来个顺 口溜(12) 脱口秀(13)？

Chinese Prime Minister Wen Jiabao likes to cite from many sources from the pre-Qin Hundred Schools of Thoughts in his national and international press conferences. He also often uses poetry as a medium for the "expression of ideals". This has caused many reporters to lament that knowledge is always insufficient when you need it as many of them have to scramble to find the source and the implication of his quotes.

Recently at the opening ceremony for the "Singapore Season in London", Singapore Senior Minister Goh Chok Tong in his opening speech, quoted the English literary bard William Shakespeare to explain that Singapore must unceasingly reform and gear for innovation.

In the future, when the "Singapore Season" is promoted in big cities in China, will ministers be able to do as the Chinese do while in China? Will they be able to recite sections of meaningful Chinese ancient poetry? Or will they perform doggerel talk shows on the spot?

1. 旁　征　博　引：
páng zhēng bó yǐn

Quote copiously from many sources.

为了表示论证充足，而大量地引用材料

引用： adduction; citation; cite; citing; excerpt; quote; reference; refers to.

博： rich; plentiful; widely

广大： greatness; hugeness; immensity; largeness; vastitude; vastness.

zhū zǐ bǎi jiā

2. 诸子百家：

Pre-Qin Hundred Schools of Thoughts.

bǎi jiā zhēng míng

百家争鸣：

Contention of a hundred schools of thought.

百家：原指战国时期的儒、法、道、墨、阴阳等思想流派。

争鸣 (contend)：比喻纷纷发表意见，展开论战。现在所说的百家争鸣，是指学术上不同的学派，可以自由争论，有时候也指可以自由发表意见。

yǐ shī yán zhì

3. 以诗言志：

Use poetry as a medium for the "expression of ideals".

以诗歌来表达人的志向怀抱。

gǎn tàn

4. 感叹：

sigh with feeling 因为有所感触而叹息。

shū dào yòng shí fāng hèn shǎo

5. 书到用时方恨少

1. Knowledge is always insufficient when you need to use it.

2. Only when knowledge was in need did I learn how little I have learnt.

chá xún

6. 查询：

question; interrogate; inquire about 查考询问。

7. 出 处：
_{chū chù}

derivation; provenance; source

典 故 (literary quotation; classical allusion)
_{diǎn gù}

成 语 (idiom; set phrase)
_{chéng yǔ}

资 料 (information; data; datum)
_{zī liào}

说 法 (parlance) 的原始 (original) 作品。
_{shuō fǎ}

8. 寓 意：
_{yù yì}

implied meaning; moral; message 寄托或蕴含的意旨或意思。

寓 言：fable; allegory; parable
_{yù yán}

9. 引 用：
_{yǐn yòng}

quote; cite; excerpt; reference; refers to

说话或写文章时借用他人作品中的词句或说法。

10. 入 乡 随 俗：
_{rù xiāng suí sú}

While in Rome, do as the Romans do

到一个地方就顺从那个地方的风俗习惯和安排。

11. 雋 永：
juàn yǒng

meaningful; fine 意味深长，引人入胜

雋：outstanding

本义：鸟肉肥美，味道好。

12. 顺 口 溜：
shùn kǒu liū

doggerel

民间的一种口头韵文，句子长短不等，纯用口语。

13. 脱 口 秀：
tuō kǒu xiù

talk show

脱口而出：bolt; blurt out; say without thinking; let slip; blunder out.

随口说出。

Table Showing New Vocabulary Learnt

zhong xin (41)	重心	centre of gravity
zhong xing (11)	中兴	resurgence
zhong yan (12)	忠言	sincere advice
zhong yan yuan (134)	中研院	Academia Sinica 中央研究院
zhong yao (44)	重药	strong medicine
zhong yi yuan (314)	众议院	House of Representatives
zhong you yi ri (1311)	终有一日	there is the time finally
zhong yu (12)	终于	at last; in the end
zhong yuan jie (122)	中元节	the Ghost Festival on the 15th day of the seventh moon
zhong z (43)	种子	seed
zhong zhi ye (424)	种植业	plantation
zhou dao (14)	周到	thoughtful; considerate
zhou mi (14)	周密	careful; thorough
zhou qi xing (114)	周期性	periodicity cyclicity
zhou ran (42)	骤然	suddenly; abruptly
zhou wei (12)	周围	around; round about =周遭
zhou xin (21)	轴心	axis
zhou xuan (12)	周旋	deal with; mix with other people
zhou ye (44)	昼夜	day and night
zhou you (12)	周游	travel around
zhou you lie guo (1242)	周游列国	travel to many countries
zhou zao (11)	周遭	around; round about =周围
zhou zhuan (13)	周转	have enough to meet the need; turnover
zhu (1)	诛	root out; kill
zhu (1)	诸	all; various
zhu (3)	嘱	advise; urge 嘱咐
zhu bi (33)	主笔	editor in chief
zhu bu (24)	逐步	progessively; step by step

（二）

在我们还没有训练足够的技师、工程师和经理人员之前，人才的短缺就必须由外籍人员来填补。虚假的自豪感并没有阻止我们聘用训练有素与经验丰富的外国专才。

经过一段相当的时期之后，国立大学、南洋理工学院和工艺学院将把每一个具有天赋的新加坡人，训练成为技师、工程师和经理人员。我们将教育每一个新加坡人，使他们都能够人尽其才。为了发挥各人的潜能，通晓第一语文是绝对必要的；通晓第二语文将使一个人有全面均衡的发展：一方面深受亚洲价值观念的薰陶，另一方面，又有西方的科学工艺技术。

1. 填补 fill (a vacancy, gap)

2. 虚假的自豪感 a false sense of pride

3. 有素 have a solid fundation (said of training)

4. 天赋 talent

5. 发挥潜能 fully bring out latent potentialities

6. 均衡 balanced, harmonious

7. 薰陶 nurture, influence (by good example, ideal, etc.)

A reading material MM Lee used in the early days — *zhu yin fu hao* was used to help pronounce unfamiliar words.

一. 请把甲组和乙组的词配搭起来:

乙组
- 文載
- 不堪设想
- 结 论
- 扭转过来
- 良好的习惯
- 产 品
- 人 才
- 人 民
- 人 才 荒

甲组
把趋势
物色
差了
后果
得出
养成
闹
质量好的
素质好的

二. 请填上适当的词:

1. 申请的人倒是很多, 但第一流的申请人却寥寥无几, ___简直___ 是屈指可数。

2. 如果我们想靠运气, 听其自然发展, ___就___ 有可能把新加坡交在一批平庸之辈的手里。___那就/那是___ 由这一批庸才和投机主义者执政五年, 大概是组成一个联合政府, 新加坡就要跪地求饶。

3. 我国的工业计划随着开始推行, 步伐 ___虽然___ 缓慢, 但却十分稳健。

4. 陈作我们能够向有才干的年轻人灌输爱国心和自尊心, 并成功地使他们产生热爱同胞的献身精神, ___然/否则___, 我们可能失去这些精英份子。

5. 这 621 名新加坡训练出来的而在澳洲注册执业的医生, 其中有 192 人的名字还保留在我国的注册执业医生的名册上。他们在澳洲注册, 是 ___为了___ 预防万一。

Language exercise.

练　习

1. 有些工作，我们可以向别的国家学习，不必另起 _炉灶_ 。　　　　*lú zào*

炉 stove
灶 kitchen range

2. 他有才干，工作认真，受到上级的 _赏识_ 。

3. 不健全的 _擢升_ 制度，是造成教师士气低落的原因之一。　　*zhuó shēng*

4. 向日本学习，培养 _敬_ 业乐 _业_ 的精神，使我国成功地进行经济重组。

5. 他是大公无私的，不会 _袒护_ 任何犯了错误的人。　　*tǎn hù*

6. 他虽然工作经验不多，但 _天赋_ 很高，可以好好地培养。（天资）　　*fù*

7. 他对党、对国家，都是忠心 _耿耿_ 的。　　*gěng gěng*

8. 狐狸 _恭维_ 乌鸦唱歌唱得好。　　*gōng wéi*

9. 黄鼠狼说：我今天来给您拜年，就是为了表示 _悔改_ 的。　　*huǐ gǎi*

10. 黄鼠狼心神 _不定_ 地问四周望望，当它看到连个人影也没有的时候，才 _镇静_ 下来。

11. 依样画 _葫芦_ 。　battle gourd　*hú lu*

12. 津津 _乐_ 道　*jīn*

13. 记忆 _犹_ 新　still　*yóu*

14. 提心 _吊胆_ 。　吊 hang, suspend　*diào dǎn*
胆 gallbladder

15. 总理访问中国，受到 _殷勤_ 的招待。　*yīn qín*

Language exercise.

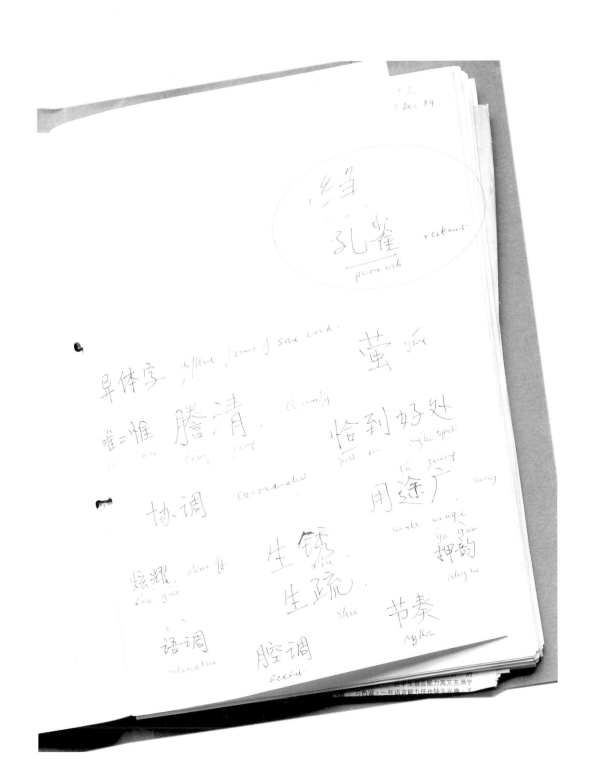

Lee Kuan Yew's Chinese hand-writing.

rom Whom

DESTRUCTION GRA

Date | To | Date | To | Date | To

...ecdotes

...ster extends to ...he moat

wind was strong.
...n the fire began
...spread to Chi's
...he and every-
...g inside was re-
...d to ashes.
...en the fire was
...and in a moment
...ck and hasti-
...e could not find

his way out and
perished.
This story originated
from a Chinese say-
ing: "The disaster ex-
tends to the fishes in
the moat," which is
used to describe how
innocent bystanders
can be affected by
problems
not of th...

油...

PAGE ONE QUOTATIONS

夫过者，大贤所不
免：然不害其为大贤者
，为其能收也。

——王守仁

Faults cannot be com-
pletely avoided even by a
man of virtues; yet
because of his ability to
reform does not pr...
him from being...
virtues.

纽约时报-专稿 **The New York Times**

日本工商界怨声载道

饭田永一、吉田广文　合撰　　　　朱成发译

在日圆升值，日货售价"水涨船高"的困境中，日本工商界一片怨声
载道。

经团连、三井、东芝和日钢管等巨型商业机构，纷纷口诛笔伐，而矛
头都指向"颟顸无能"的中曾根政府，这些机构均束手无策，到处弥
漫悲观气氛。　　　　　　　　　　　　　　　　　　　　——译者按

另一方面，对於日圆汹涌澎湃的涨势，这些机构均束手无策，到处弥

日圆节节上升，毫无止境的局面，使日本
工商界领袖一筹莫展。在无计可施之余，他们
迁怒于中曾根政府，指责政府"颟顸无能"，
无力制止工商业的下降趋势。

工业家和出口商，对于中曾根的能力已丧失
信心。中曾根最近下令采取"果敢措施"。但
对于这些没有说明具体做法的工商措施，工商界领
...此...在中曾根下令前一天，1美元兑
...日圆大关。

所带来的强大冲击，或是主动减低出口。"

工商界领袖一般认为，1美元兑159日
圆的涨势"极不寻常"。他们愤慨地指出，日
圆的高币值，已超出了日本工商界力挽颓势的
能力。

美元兑率还会暴跌

日本商工会议所所长乡渡同意这种看法。
他说，以目前这种全球经济带来"极度恶劣"的影
响突然暴跌，给全球经济干预汇率的时候了

Some Useful Resources for Chinese Language Learning

A. Compact Discs/Chinese Software

1) Kingsoft's PowerWord 2005 (金山词霸)

A Chinese and English learning, translation and dictionary software. When users highlight or point to an unfamiliar word using the mouse, there are instant translations and pronunciation. There is also an input field for search purposes. The input type can be in English, simplified or traditional Chinese. The smart lookup engine encompasses information from 200 dictionaries and 80 professional wordbanks.

2) *Zhong Hua Chuan Shi Cang Shu* (《中华传世藏书》)

A huge encyclopedia of Chinese classical literature, it contains five compact discs featuring classics by the pre-*Qin* thinkers, works on Buddhism, Taoism, military strategies, Tang and Song poetry, as well as the modern literary works (including poems, prose and essays), among others.

3) Interactive Practical *Pu Tong Hua* (电脑互动实用普通话) (Chinese-English)

An interactive programme targetting professionals, it includes basic knowledge on Mandarin pronunciation, lessons, vocabulary and games.

4) Chinese Plus 2004

This software contains the following features:

- English-Chinese Input Method

  Allows user to input Chinese characters by typing their equivalent English words. For example, by typing "embed", the Chinese character 嵌入 will appear.

- PowerWord

  A Chinese-English electronic dictionary that provides the user with the pronunciation, meaning and the usage of Chinese and English language instantly. The user can simply point the mouse to an unfamiliar Chinese character and its meaning will pop-up instantly. The programme can read the character aloud too.

- Stroke Star

  An animated Chinese character stroke sequence program, it demonstrates how the most common 3000 Chinese characters should be written.

- *Han yu pin yin* auto add-on

  It helps to add-on *han yu pin yin* symbols automatically to any Chinese character freely at any position decided by the user.

B. Websites

1) cb.kingsoft.com (詞霸搜索)

An online version of the PowerWord dictionary software, it provides free search of words that the PowerWord holds in its wordbank.

2) zh.wikipedia.org

A free encyclopedia in over 50 languages. Its Chinese version was started in October 2002 and now contains some 23,000 items.

3) wordpedia.britannica.com/concise

Britannica Concise Encyclopedia (online) contains some 7.5 million Chinese-English explanations.

4) Translation Websites

a) www.worldlingo.com/wl/MSTranslate

b) chineseterms.zaobao.com/chineseterms.html

  A website put up by the Translation Standardisation Committee for the Chinese Media which was set up in Singapore in 1990 for the purpose of standardising Chinese translations of commonly used terms in the country's Chinese media.

The current website features the major works of the Committee, which include the following:

- Singapore government departmental titles and designations;
- Names of companies and organisations;
- Names of personalities and places;
- Names of buildings and housing estates;
- Bilingual computer/financial terms;
- Malaysian/Indonesian names in Chinese.

c) www.chinatranslation.net/gjjg.asp

A site featuring the official translation of names of government agencies, hospitals, universities, resources and others in China.

d) www.lcsd.gov.hk/CE/Museum/Space/Research/StarName/c_research_chinengstars.htm

A Chinese-English astrology translation.

e) www.sinoexam.cn/interactive/translation

An interactive English-Chinese/Chinese-English translation website that offers translation of literary works and tips on translation.

5) Downloading Software to Display Chinese Text

a) www.zaobao.com.sg/pages/zbhelp.html

b) chinese.yahoo.com/docs/info/download.html

6) Search Engines

a) www.google.com.sg

b) dir.sogou.com

7) Literary Resources

a) cls.admin.yzu.edu.tw/HOME.HTM

Developed based on the concept of having a library without walls, the website contains links to information on Chinese classics, poems, important conferences and even online pedagogy.

b) www.lib.washington.edu/East-asia/china/chinaindex.html

University of Washington East Asia Library's Index to Chinese Classic Literature on the Internet.

c) www.xys.org/library.html

Xin Yu Si Electronic Library (新语丝电子文库) is a public FTP archive site dedicated to storing electronic versions (GB code) of Chinese literatures. It mainly stores XYS magazines and Chinese classics. It is currently the most complete public archive site of Chinese classics and has six divisions:

- XYS magazine: stores GB, HZ, Big5, and PS versions of all issues of XYS magazine.
- XYS-friends archives: stores the posters posted in xys-friends mailing list.
- Chinese classics: currently it has seven subdivisions: philosophy, classical poetry, classical proses, classical novels, classical criticism, classical erotica, and Lu Xun's works.
- Electronic ebooks: it has two subdivisions: Modern Literature and Others. The Modern Literature collects the works by modern writers and poets, while the Others collects the works of philosophy, history, and religion.
- Chinese netters' works: selectively stores the works by Chinese netters active in alt.chinese.text, xys-friends and chpoem-l.
- Chinese netters' pictures: stores Chinese netters' digital pictures.

d) www.chineselib.com

Chinese library, contains information on authors, Chinese-English dictionary, etc.

8) Chinese Language Learning

a) llt.msu.edu

Language Learning & Technology: a refereed journal for second and foreign language educators.

b) www.china-language.gov.cn

A website established by the language writing application research institute with China's Ministry of Education. It features:

- www.china-language.gov.cn/weblaw/index.asp
  News highlights on language issues, language policies, rules and regulations of Chinese character standardisation.

- www.china-language.gov.cn/xinxi/index.asp
  Information on academic language workshops and papers.

- www.china-language.gov.cn/jgsz/pth/index.html
  The *pu tong hua* [普通话, literally common speech of the Chinese language] test centre which is responsible for the training, examination and research on *pu tong hua* at the national level.

c) center.ecnu.edu.cn/HW

News on teaching Chinese as a foreign language.

9) Media

Lianhe Zaobao: www.zaobao.com

Todayonline: www.todayonline.com

MediaCorp's Channel 8: ch8c.mediacorptv.com

MediaCorp's Channel 5: ch5.mediacorptv.com

Channel News Asia (Chinese): www.cna.tv/index_gb.htm

Channel News Asia (English): www.channelnewsasia.com

Phoenix TV: www.phoenixtv.com/phoenixtv

Yes933 radio station: yes933.mediacorpradio.com

Capital 95.8FM: capital958.mediacorpradio.com

Love 972: love972.mediacorpradio.com

Radio Singapore International: rsi.mediacorpradio.com

UFM1003: www.ufm1003.com

Safra Radio (Dongli 88.3): dongli883.com.sg

Xinhua Net: www.xinhua.org

Mandarin Daily News (targetted at children): www.mdnkids.com

10) www.mandarin.org.sg

Website for the Speak Mandarin Campaign which was launched by then Prime Minister Mr Lee Kuan Yew in 1979. Now into its 26th year, the campaign is a year-round campaign, focusing on creating awareness through publicity and getting community involvement. Several programmes to facilitate the learning of Mandarin have been introduced. These include publications/ resources such as CD-ROMs and tapes of Mandarin lessons for people who are keen to learn Mandarin, handbooks of English-Chinese terms and telephone Mandarin lessons.

11) www.sfcca.org.sg

Website of Singapore Federation of Chinese Clan Associations. Apart from news on the federation and its member clan associations, it carries information on important Chinese festivals, Chinese names of temples, schools, hospitals, banks, etc.

12) www.nmch.gov.cn

The National Museum of China.

13) zhongwen.com

Zhongwen.com contains the complete text of the Chinese-English dictionary, *Chinese Characters: A Genealogy and Dictionary*, which uses the new *zi pu* [字谱, system of character trees].

- zhongwen.com/zi.htm

  Chinese Characters Dictionary Web: The major Chinese character dictionaries on the web are interlinked at a character-to-character level, allowing visitors to quickly cross from one dictionary to another (more than a dozen of them that spread across seven countries and four continents), to check the same character entry without having to search again for the character.

14) www.chineselanguage.org

A website with information on the Chinese languages including dialects.

15) www.mandarintools.com/family.html

A website on Chinese family titles.

16) edu.ocac.gov.tw

Global Chinese language and culture; it provides resources (e.g., songs, riddles, phrases, etc.,) for students of different levels, as well as the simulated online Chinese proficiency test and a glimpse into the Chinese culture (folklore, stories, sayings, etc.), among others.

17) 192.192.169.101/et/home.htm

Taiwan's National Institute of Educational Resources and Research.

18) learning.edu.tw

Set up by Taiwan's Education Ministry, it carries information on six learning areas: nature, arts, health, science, culture and life.

19) www.EdnoLand.com/ChineseLearning

A Chinese language learning website for young children, it features proper methods of teaching Chinese such as grouping words with related shapes and roots to further enhance their learning. Interactive learning tools incorporating these methods are included to create a stimulating Chinese learning environment and effectively engage this generation of children.

20) wise.edu.tw/lifelong/study-links.htm

A list of Taiwan's bookclubs.

C. Dictionaries/Handbooks

1) The Contemporary Chinese Dictionary (Chinese-English Edition, 2002, Foreign Language Teaching and Research Press) (《现代汉语词典》, 2002 年增补本，汉英双语)

This dictionary sets out to popularise standard Chinese and standardise its vocabulary. It also includes words from classical times that have survived in contemporary usage as well as slang and words from Chinese dialects that have become widely used. It puts together a compendium of every day words, encyclopedia of terms of standard reference, definitions and illustrative examples.

2) *Xin Hua Xin Ci Yu Ci Dian* (2003) 《新华新词语词典》

Edited and published by Commercial Press, it collates all new and "hip" phrases that have surfaced between 1990 and 2002. It carries some 2200 such phrases and 4000 related expressions. The phrases are classified under different sections: finance and economics, environmental protection, medicine, sports, military, science and technology, commonly-used words like "the clone", "win-win" and so on. For the convenience of English-speaking users, English translations of the phrases are also included.

3) *A New English-Chinese Dictionary of Idioms* (2004) 《新英汉成语词典》

Contains some 40,000 commonly-used expressions found in English literature, news reports, academic papers and colloquial language.

4) *Pu Tong Hua Shui Ping Ce Shi Shi Shi Gang Yao* (《普通话水平测试实施纲要》**, or translated as A Handbook on Standard Mandarin Test)**

A handbook on the requirements of the Standard Mandarin Test in China, it features a lexicon table (containing 17,055 phrases), comparison of Mandarin with dialects, articles for oratorical purpose (60 of them) and topics for conversations (30 topics).

D. Others

magnifier.sourceforge.net

Featuring the Virtual Magnifying Glass 2.35 which is a free, open source, screen magnification tool for Windows.

Epilogue

Ho Sheo Be

You rise to thank him repeatedly for spending two afternoons under the glare of tungsten lights, flashing megawatt smiles that you think are exclusive to a celebrity wannabe. But Lee Kuan Yew, the lifelong learner, is quick to dismiss it.

"Everything would be worthwhile if I can set a good example for others to follow and encourage them to learn Chinese," says the statesman, Singapore's Minister Mentor.

Coming from a mature language learner who began to seriously pick up Mandarin only at the age of 32, and has continued to do so for the past 50 years, such words are certainly encouraging.

The name "Lee Kuan Yew" immediately came to mind when a decision was made to publish a book that promotes the learning of Mandarin, one of the most commonly used languages in the world, but one which is slowly losing its grounds with Singaporean Chinese.

The initial idea was a simple one — put together an interview (possibly an email interview that the busy political leader could manage at his own time) plastered with archived photographs and quotations drawn from his past speeches on the subject of speaking or learning Mandarin.

Unfortunately (or rather fortunately), the opportune moment to put forth the request to MM Lee did not arise until an overhaul of the pedagogy of Chinese language was announced in late 2004. To ride on a renewed interest in the language, the net was immediately cast to fish for advice from MM Lee's Chinese tutors, press secretary and Mandarin-speaking Members of Parliament with whom he practises Mandarin.

A more comprehensive learning package subsequently took shape — notes and reading materials MM Lee has painstakingly collected over the years can be featured too, not forgetting the software that the English-educated finds useful in relating Mandarin to his master language.

What followed was a concept paper on the learning package. Little did you expect that the avid learner, reputed for seizing every opportunity to attend Chinese tuition classes, would sacrifice two such sessions for a face-to-face interview and agree to the recording of the process into an eBook so that messages can be put forth more convincingly.

So, when the eventful day for the interview arrives and your heels set off the alarm at the Istana's point of security clearance, your heart literally races. You would not want all the earlier preparations to go down the drain and would even leave the shoes at the security to prove your innocence. Of course, no such demand is made!

Works of Chinese calligraphy — a testimony to MM Lee's love for the Chinese language and culture — quickly greet your eyes as you walk along the corridor leading to his office. Just as you assume his office would boast of the same "Chinese-ness", you discover it is not a lens man's dream. Not only is it not adorned with Chinese rosewood antique furnishing or Chinese landscape paintings and delicate crafts given by the world's who's who, the wooden stand on which his reading materials rest looks so coarse and the recorder he uses to record his Mandarin conversations so archaic that you think you could have entered the wrong office.

Still, the video and photography crew put up their equipment promptly, raring to capture MM Lee's images for posterity, and as if too happy to take a leaf from an important lesson on MM Lee's "Pragmatism 101".

And when the "protagonist" appears half an hour before the slated time, repeating "ye hao" [也好, fine too] to all of your suggestions as if he is sure things are left in good hands, you know the work would be a breeze. The Minister Mentor at the two interview sessions for this work is indeed the kind of interviewee any journalist would die for.

"Never mind that tape, it won't fall off," he tells the soundman who is too keen to secure the microphone onto his shirt with a masking tape. He then goes on to ask for his working chair that he is most comfortable in — a legitimate request, you reckon.

The consummate speaker knows exactly where and when to raise his voice or make powerful pauses to stress his points. He listens to your questions attentively and does not quiz any of them — contradicting what you have been forewarned. Often, his replies dissolve into laughter, exuding such an amicable air that the photographer who captures his candid gestures is worried those who are more familiar with MM Lee's serious demeanour would not identify with this less known disposition.

Admittedly, MM Lee neither speaks flawless Mandarin with a Beijing accent nor expounds aphorisms akin to what a scholar does. However, the relentless effort to grasp Mandarin more than compensates.

As you listen to the 82-year-old read a Chinese newspaper article aloud, under your request, correcting his mistakes and raising questions on the content of the article earnestly, you bite your lower lip to contain an imminent cough that would otherwise cause a distraction. You decide to keep intact in the DVD that accompanies this book some Chinese characters that MM Lee has pronounced wrongly during the interview in Mandarin, not to ridicule the man but to display his genuine intent in walking his talk.

Never mind that you have heard tales about how MM Lee chides reporters for turning up at events in jeans or how he demands his tea or office to be kept at a particular temperature, the only displeasure you observe over the two afternoons is a reminder to his guards to get the handrail besides a flight of stairs repainted as he mounts them.

You will constantly be reminded of how MM Lee knits his brows and avoids your eyes as he speaks of the "deep sense of loss" he had when he could not speak Mandarin. You are convinced that such fear that his countrymen would one day share this deprivation prompts MM Lee to bring to the open an experience that would have otherwise gone unnoticed.